Fertility in Asia

Fertility in Asia: Assessing the Impact of Development Projects

Edited by
John Stoeckel and
Anrudh K. Jain,
The Populaton Council

St. Martin's Press, New York

Scholarly & Reference Division,
St. Martin's Press, Inc., 175 Fifth Avenue, New York, NY 10010

First published in the United States of America in 1986

Printed in Great Britain

ISBN 0-312-00078-2

Library of Congress Cataloging-in-Publication Data

Fertility in Asia.
Includes bibliographies and index.
1. Fertility, Human—Asia—Case studies.
2. Economic development projects—Asia—Case studies. I. Stoeckel, John E. II. Jain, Anrudh K.
HB1043.A3F47 1986 304.6'32'095 86-17838
ISBN 0-312-00078-2

Table of Contents

List of Figures

List of Tables

Foreword

From time to time and place to place the assertion is made that 'development is the best contraceptive.' When I joined the Population Council at the start of 1976, that slogan was still ringing in the ears of many who had attended the International Conference on Population in Bucharest in 1974. In his major address at the Forum attached to that conference, John D. Rockefeller 3rd, founder of the Population Council in 1952 and its chairman for 25 years, expressed his personal disappointment that family planning programs had not been more successful and called for a '... probing reappraisal of all that has been done in the population field, all that has been learned, so that the years ahead may yield the results mankind so desperately wants.'

Of course, everyone knew that the so-called developed countries, the richer and technologically more advanced nations of Europe, North America, Oceania and Japan, had low rates of population growth characterized by low fertility and low mortality. And everyone knew, too, that the high population growth rates in what we call the developing countries, the poorer countries of Africa, Asia and Latin America characterized by low per capita incomes and low technologies of production, were generally a result of mortality reduction without corresponding changes in fertility. Relatively cheap and highly effective life-saving technologies from developed countries had been used in developing ones, but without corresponding birth reductions.

The response from the community of developed country donors active in supporting efforts to raise the levels of income and wealth in the developing countries was to back a new set of inputs specifically designed to reduce fertility: family planning programs, the organized and subsidized delivery by governments and non-governmental organizations of contraceptive services along with efforts to teach about them and motivate people to use them. This response was driven by concern that rapid population growth in poor countries would too easily absorb the slow-maturing fruits of development efforts, leaving everyone as poor, or poorer, after several years of investment and effort as they had been at the start. As President Lyndon Johnson of the United States of America urged a United Nations audience in 1965: 'Let us act on the fact that less than five dollars invested in population control is worth a hundred dollars invested in economic growth.' It was against this line of thinking that several respected developing country delegations rebelled at Bucharest.

Historically, shifts in the now developed countries from high to low regimes of fertility and mortality occurred over periods ranging from 100 to 200 years and lagged behind their shifts from low to higher technologies of production and per capita incomes. If the world were to take literally the argument that 'development is the best contraceptive,' how could there ever be enough development attained within some reasonable future period to produce the 'automatic' fertility reductions experienced earlier in Europe? Under current circumstances in the developing countries, as distinguished from historical ones in the now developed countries, rapidly growing populations were likely to absorb development advances as fast or faster than they could be achieved. My predecessor as president of the Population Council, Bernard Berelson, put that argument in 1978 with characteristic trenchancy:

> 'the objective of the whole exercise is to expedite that [fertility] reduction in order to hasten development; so recommending the latter as a way to achieve the former really misses the point.'

Nevertheless, the Third World expressions at Bucharest did not go unheard. In the United States one response was embodied in a 1976 amendment to the Foreign Assistance Act, section 104(d), quoted in the first chapter of this book.

At the Population Council, I stated in a paper prepared for our Board of Trustees within months after joining:

> More than 97 percent of the world's development budgets are spent on subjects designated as other than 'population programs.' A population lens is hardly ever used to study these projects at any stage. A major reason is that the population lenses are still so imperfect for this purpose. The Council's policy research should produce effective and practical analytical tools through which existing and projected development processes, policies, and programs can be examined so that their population impacts can be better understood.

Shortly after that, the Council initiated a project in which we sought to learn whether specific development projects had measurable impacts on fertility. The present volume distills the research output of that project.

Beyond the generalizations that once a country was 'developed' its fertility would moderate 'automatically,' one always sensed that specific development inputs were not likely to be fertility-neutral. That is to say, if they transformed people's lives economically and socially they were likely, too, to affect desires about family size. Could it not be possible, then, to design these projects—in sectors other than population and undertaken with objectives other than demographic—so that their fertility impacts would tend in the direction prescribed by national policy, downward in many developing countries? The task is by no means simple, nor the effects direct or short term, but the work reported here gives promise that, indeed, practical steps towards this end are possible.

The essays collected in this volume report on cross-sectional research, that is, studies of information collected at a single moment in time. These studies provide, for the first time, an empirical demonstration of how development projects operate through a series of intermediate factors to affect fertility. Acknowledging that the results of such fertility impact studies will seldom be useful for making investment choices among development projects (since these projects will probably continue to be justified on their projected development impacts alone), Drs. Stoeckel and Jain draw several broad implications for population-related development policy. The editors also highlight methodological issues encountered in assessing the impact of development upon fertility. This contribution to the knowledge base about population and development will be of keen interest to concerned academicians, policy-makers, and program managers.

A next step will be to perfect appraisals that assess likely fertility impacts in advance and, thus, allow for design modifications to be made during the project formulation process.

George Zeidenstein,
President
The Population Council
New York, N.Y.
May 1986

Preface

At the 1974 World Population Conference held in Bucharest, developing country delegates emphasized the role of development as 'the best contraceptive.' At the 1984 Conference in Mexico, however, it was the United States who emphasized the role of economic advancement in decreasing the rate of population growth in developing countries. While those involved in the debate in international forums have changed their positions, the emphasis on development as a means to reduce the rate of population growth persisted during the decade.

Whether development will reduce fertility in developing countries is not the issue. The issues are what type of development will reduce fertility, by how much, in what time period, and what can governments do to accelerate the process of change. A number of efforts have been made since the mid 1970s to address these issues, in particular to generate scientific knowledge concerning interrelationships between development and population processes, and to incorporate this knowledge in the development planning process in LDCs. This book is an outgrowth of one such effort—a program on the Fertility Impacts of Development (FID) in Asia—initiated by the Population Council in 1978. The focus of this book is on the quantification of the impact of development on fertility.

The FID program, managed by the Council's regional office in Bangkok, Thailand, was originally designed to improve the communication of policy-relevant research on the impact of development on fertility behavior to policy makers and program planners in Asia. The specific objective of this program was to expand support for research activities directed at achieving a better understanding of the critical and policy-relevant population and development interactions and to give attention to ways of translating that understanding into actionable programs.

Four types of activities were undertaken to achieve the basic objective of the FID program:

1. A studies program to support research by Asian scholars on the quantification of the fertility impacts of development processes and programs;
2. A series of policy and technical workshops to stimulate research proposals, to share research experience, and to stimulate interactions among the researchers and policy makers;
3. Provision of technical assistance to development planners and policy makers in Asia, in order to develop programs that give explicit attention to their fertility impacts; and
4. Dissemination of information to researchers and policy makers in Asia through publications resulting from studies, workshops, and technical assistance.

This book presents the results of five selected studies funded under the 'studies program.' Three of these studies, two in Thailand and one in Sri Lanka, focused upon the fertility effects of interventions to improve economic conditions. These interventions include agricultural irrigation, rural electrification, land settlement, and a guaranteed minimum price scheme. The remaining two projects examine the fertility effects of female employment in industrial and non-industrial settings in the Philippines, and the fertility effects of child labor and schooling in India.

Each of these five empirical studies is presented as a separate chapter in this book. The opening chapter presents an overview of the major findings of these studies and their implications for population policy and further research; and the concluding chapter discusses the methodological issues encountered in attempting to assess the fertility impacts of development.

While policy makers could, theoretically, consider potential impacts of development on fertility during the planning process, such explicit considerations are rarely made. Among the reasons for this lack of consideration is the absence of empirical information required to quantify the fertility impacts of development. This book starts to fill this gap in knowledge and provides for the first time an empirical demonstration of the linkage between development and fertility; thus expanding the knowledge base on the interrelationships which, we hope, will be of substantial interest to professionals—researchers and policy-makers alike—in the field of population and development.

We are grateful to the researchers who have contributed to this volume. Following suggestions given by their colleagues and Council staff at workshops on further data analysis, the researchers expanded and refined the analysis of data from their projects and revised their work accordingly. Recognition must also be given to J. Jarrett Clinton and Barnett F. Baron for their contribution at the formative stages of the design and development of the FID program. We would like to thank Dorothy Meyer, who meticulously typed several drafts of the book.

The research on which the studies included in this book are based was supported by a grant to the Population Council by the United States Agency for International Development. The book would not have been completed without the support of other donors to the Population Council, including the William and Flora Hewlett and Andrew W. Mellon Foundations and the Japan Shipbuilding Industry Foundation. The views expressed in this book are the contributors' own and do not necessarily reflect those of the organizations to which they belong or of the donor agencies who supported the project.

John Stoeckel Anrudh K. Jain

List of Contributors

1 **Dr Michael A. Costello**, sociologist, is an Associate Professor of Sociology at Xavier University, Philippines. After graduating from the University of Notre Dame, he obtained a doctorate in sociology from the University of Chicago. His research interests include 'Women in Development' and determinants of fertility in the Philippines. He has conducted several seminars on sociology, statistical analysis, and social science research in the United States and the Philippines.

2 **Dr Anrudh K. Jain**, sociologist-demographer, is Senior Associate and Deputy Director, International Programs, the Population Council. After graduating from Delhi University, he obtained a doctorate in sociology from the University of Michigan. He has had extensive experience in working with professionals and institutions in developing countries; in managing large-scale data sets; in the analysis and evaluation of family planning programs; in assessing the fertility impacts of development projects; in demographic analysis of census and sample survey (e.g., World Fertility Survey) data; and in developing and using mathematical models. As Deputy Director of International Programs he assists the Director in program development and management of the Council's activities overseas.

3 **Ramesh Kanbargi** received his master's degree in sociology from Karnatak University, Karnataka, India. He is currently Research Investigator in the Population Research Centre of the Institute for Social and Economic Change, Bangalore, India. His research interests include fertility and family planning use in India.

4 **Dr P. M. Kulkarni**, statistician-demographer, is a Fellow at the Population Research Centre, Institute for Social and Economic

Change, Bangalore, India. After graduating from Shivaji University, he obtained a doctorate in statistics from Colorado State University and completed a post-doctoral fellowship at Brown University. His research interests include infant mortality, fertility, and family planning.

5 **Dr Marilou Palabrica-Costello**, sociologist, is Associate Professor and Chairman, Department of Sociology and Anthropology, Xavier University, Philippines. After graduating from Xavier University, she obtained a doctorate in sociology from the University of Chicago. Her research interests include 'Women in Development', rural–urban mobility, employment, and fertility in the Philippines.

6 **Dr Suwanlee Piampiti**, sociologist-demographer, is Associate Professor and Dean of the School of Applied Statistics at the National Institute of Development Administration in Thailand. After graduating from Chulalongkorn University, she obtained a doctorate in sociology from the University of Georgia. Her research interests include internal migration and 'Women and Development' in Thailand.

7 **Dr Suchart Prasith-rathsint**, sociologist-demographer, is an Associate Professor in Applied Statistics at the National Institute of Development Administration in Thailand. After graduating from Victoria University, New Zealand, he obtained a doctorate in sociology from Brown University. He has published several textbooks on statistics and edited a volume on micro-level studies in 'Population and Development' in Thailand.

8 **Laddawan Roodmanee**, received her master's degree from Mahidol University, Thailand. She is currently a Lecturer in the Faculty of Social Science and Humanities, National Institute of Development Administration, Thailand. Her research interests include mortality and development.

9 **Dr N. L. Sirisena**, economist, is Chief Statistician, Statistics Branch of Central Bank of Sri Lanka. He is also the Director of Social Science Research Council in Colombo. After obtaining his M.A. in Agriculture Economics from the University of

Manchester, Dr Sirisena obtained a Certificate in Public Administration and Planning from the University of Oslo and doctorate in Development Economics from IDS at the University of Sussex. He has conducted national socio-economic surveys in Sri Lanka as well as regional socio-economic surveys under the Mahavelli project in Sri Lanka.

10 **Dr Kanikar Sookasame**, sociologist-demographer is an Assistant Professor in the School of Applied Statistics, National Institute of Development Administration in Thailand. After graduating from Chulalongkorn University, she obtained a doctorate in sociology from Utah State University. Her research interests include fertility, mortality and "women in development" in Thailand.

11 **Manu Srikhajon**, received his post-graduate diploma in forestry from Kasetsart University, Thailand. He is a senior staff member of the Department of Land Development, Government of Thailand. His interests include water resource development and population.

12 **Dr John Stoeckel**, sociologist-demographer, is a Senior Associate with the Population Council stationed at the Council's South and East Asia Regional Office in Bangkok, Thailand. Dr Stoeckel obtained his doctorate from Michigan State University. He has lived and worked in a number of Asian countries working on fertility and mortality research and FP/MCH project evaluation. He had major responsibility for substantive and management direction of the Council's Fertility Impacts of Development Project in Asia, and is currently responsible for the direction and management of the Council's Research Program on Infant and Child Survival in Thailand.

1 Introduction and Overview

John Stoeckel and Anrudh K. Jain

Introduction

The interdependence between population growth and socio-economic development has been recognized in the demographic literature for a long time. Numerous studies have focussed not only on the consequences of population growth but also on its determinants. These studies made important contributions in shaping population policies which culminated in the implementation of nationally organized family planning programs during the 1960s as the main intervention to reduce the rate of population growth in developing countries.

Following the Bucharest Conference in 1974, the population field in general and a number of international organizations including The Population Council went through a period during which the basic premise underlying population activities was re-examined. This re-examination led to a number of attempts to fully integrate population concerns in development planning. In 1976, for example, the Foreign Assistance Act was amended by the United States Congress to include Section 104(d) which states that

> Assistance under this Chapter shall be administered so as to give particular attention to the interrelationship between (A) population growth, and (B) development and overall improvement in living standards in developing countries, and to the impact of all programs, projects, and activities on population growth.

The United Nations Fund for Population Activities initiated steps to establish population units in planning organizations in order to facilitate the incorporation of population concerns in developmental activities.

Activities related to the incorporation of population concerns in development can be divided into two distinct groups: (1) implications of population growth for achievement of development objectives and (2) implications of development strategies for population growth. Work related to the consequences of rapid population growth and how to incorporate them in development planning has been going on since the mid-1950s and is not reviewed in this book (see for example, Coale & Hoover, 1958; McNicoll, 1984; U.N., 1985; and NRC, 1986).

Among population specialists, policy concerns regarding the impact of development on population were based on the fact that more than 97 percent of the world's development budget was spent on activities designated as other than population (family planning) programs. It was assumed that most developmental policies are not neutral with regard to their effects on demographic behavior, and that invariably they do have an effect on individual decisions about family size, spacing, and contraceptive behavior. Some might have pronatalistic effects and others antinatalistic. Policymakers could, theoretically, consider potential impacts of various alternative development policies on demographic variables during the planning process and in the selection, design and implementation of developmental activities. However, such explicit considerations were rarely made.

It was further assumed that this lack of consideration might have been, in part, due to:

1. lack of awareness about the utility of considering demographic impacts of developmental activities;
2. lack of interest because some programs, such as improved education, can be adequately justified solely on the basis of their non-demographic objectives alone;
3. lack of sound theoretical bases for establishing causal relationships between developmental inputs/outputs and changes in demographic components; and
4. lack of empirical information required to quantify the demographic impacts of specified developmental inputs.

Two types of activities were thought to be important in facilitating the incorporation of the demographic impacts of development in the planning process. First, research specific to selected developmental activities was required to improve and strengthen the knowledge base concerning the actual demographic impacts of developmental activities. This empirical information was thought to be necessary for assessing a priori the potential implications of development for population processes with increasing accuracy and efficiency. Second, it was necessary to identify processes through which knowledge about the impact of development on population, as it improves, can be integrated into the planning process and utilized in selecting, designing, and implementing developmental activities.

One of the major program initiatives undertaken by The Population Council in response to perceived needs of the field in the late 1970s was a program on the Fertility Impacts of Development (FID) in Asia. Support for this program was obtained from a grant awarded by USAID to the Council in September 1978. The overall objective of this program was to generate new knowledge about the impact of socioeconomic development on fertility and to assist policymakers and program managers in incorporating the implications of development on fertility in the planning process. This was the only program which systematically considered all aspects of 'Section 104(d)' of the United States Foreign Assistance Act.

Miro and Potter (1980) in the report of the International Review Group (IRG) also recommended support for the type of studies conducted under this program:

> Given the demand by policy-makers for studies of the fertility impact of programmes and projects that governments are now carrying out, and the belief of at least some scholars that evaluative studies can produce meaningful results, resources must be devoted to increasing the amount of effort that is devoted to this kind of research. Nevertheless, it should be recognized that theoretically and methodologically sound quasi-experimental research designs for this sort of study have yet to be developed. [Miro and Potter, 1980, pp. 113–114].

Activities under this program on the Fertility Impacts of Development in Asia had started before the publication of the IRG report and, as shown in this monograph, they made important contributions to both research methodologies and population policy.

Approaches and the Organization of the Monograph

Research activities related to the impact of development on fertility are quite similar in nature to those related to the determinants of fertility. There is one important difference, however. The investigator in the determinants type of research moves *backward* in orientation from fertility to its determinants and then to public policies and interventions. The orientation in the impact type of research, on the other hand, is *forward* from public policies and interventions to their effects on the determinants of fertility and then to fertility itself. The selection of the determinants to be used in the impact research as intervening factors between public policies and fertility, however, has to be based on the state of the determinants research.

The impact studies supported under the FID program placed an emphasis on the quantification of the effect of development processes and projects on fertility. The quantification of the impact at the *project* level rather than at the *policy* level received additional emphasis for two reasons: (i) development policies, in general, are implemented through specific programs and projects; and (ii) implementation of a policy and, therefore, its effectiveness is likely to vary from project to project. Thus a policy concerning land reform, for example, might be considered to have important fertility implications in a country. But unless it is implemented in an area, its actual effect on fertility change cannot be quantified.

An assessment of the fertility effects of development at the project level is obtained through a *fertility impact study* approach which refers to the measurement of *actual* fertility effects of inputs provided through a development project. The studies presented in Chapters 2 through 6 utilized this approach and are as follows: 'Fertility Impacts of Development Programs in Sri Lanka,' by N. L. Sirisena & J. Stoeckel; 'Fertility Effects of Electrification in Northeast Thailand,' by Suwanlee Piampiti; 'Fertility Effects of Agricultural Irrigation in Northeast Thailand,' by Suchart Prasith-rathsint, Kanikar Sookasame, Laddawan Roodmanee and Manu Srikhagorn; 'Female Employment, Occupational Setting and Fertility in a Philippine City,' by Michael Costello & Marilou Palabrica-Costello; and 'Child Labor, Schooling and Fertility in Rural Karnataka, South India,' by Ramesh Kanbargi & P. M. Kulkarni. An overview of various methodological issues involved in the assessment of the impact of development projects is presented in Chapter 7.

The remaining portion of this chapter discusses the conceptual framework, research design and level of analysis utilized in the fertility impact studies; it summarizes the major findings of the studies; compares these findings with those from related research activities; and discusses implications for further research and population policy.

Conceptual Framework

The conceptual framework selected for assessing fertility impacts of development is presented in the following diagram:

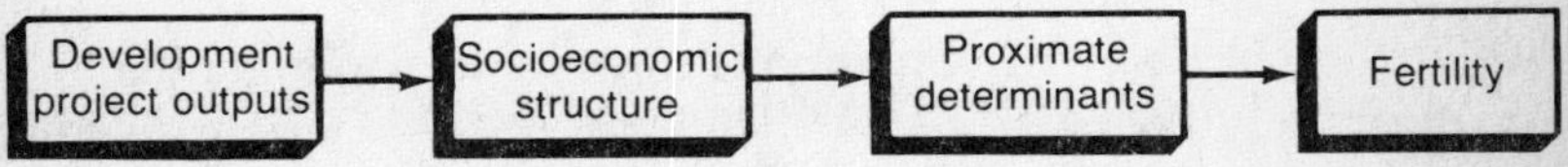

In general, the impact of development project outputs upon fertility is viewed as indirect, operating through changes in the socioeconomic structure which affect the demand for children. By improving social and economic conditions and by creating a demand for consumer goods and social services, development process is viewed as creating a demand to reduce fertility. These changes in the demand structure are translated into actual fertility through changes in the intermediate variables or the proximate determinants, especially through increased use of contraception (See Davis and Blake, 1956, for the list of 11 intermediate variables; and Bongaarts, 1978, for the four most important proximate determinants). The empirical studies included in this book utilized either all or a portion of this framework to generate hypotheses and guide their analyses. This framework, however, does not include population projects which can directly influence proximate determinants of fertility. For example, provision of family planning services in an area can increase the use of contraception and decrease fertility without changing the socioeconomic structure and demand for children. Assessment of the fertility impact of such projects is not included in this monograph.

The study in Sri Lanka on the fertility effects of electrification, land settlement and guaranteed minimum price schemes (and their combinations) and two studies conducted in Thailand on fertility effects of electrification and irrigation, respectively, utilized the total framework. These studies deal with the governmental sponsored infrastructural projects and their output is measured by the presence of these facilities in rural communities.

The remaining two studies, one conducted in the Philippines and the other in India, used a portion of the framework. These two studies do not specifically deal with the presence of a particular governmental sponsored infrastructural facility. Instead they start with the output of various governmental and non-governmental efforts to improve economic and social conditions. The Philippine study starts with the developmental setting (industrial and non-industrial) of female employment, both of which are subject to influences from broad governmental actions such as those related to foreign investment, minimum wage laws, and gender discrimination in the labor market. The Indian study starts with child schooling and child labor, both of which are influenced by governmental and private actions such as the presence of a school in the village, governmental regulations concerning child labor, and opportunities and need for children to work. As such, these two studies shed additional light on the fertility implications of governmental interventions as they operate through female employment in the Philippines and child labor and schooling in India. The conceptual frameworks and the specific variables utilized for each of the five studies are presented in the respective chapters reporting on the studies.

Study Design

Several types of study designs were considered for measuring the impact of development projects on fertility. Prospective or longitudinal studies, with or without experimental designs, were not initiated because of the time and monetary constraints. Natural experiments were not excluded but we were unable to identify experiments with baseline data on fertility along with information concerning developmental inputs. Studies focussed on countries as the unit of analysis to quantify the effects of developmental indicators on fertility were not encouraged because the high level of aggregation in such studies masks important differentials within countries (see for example, Cutright, 1983; and Mauldin & Lapham, 1984).

A cross-sectional approach which relies upon information collected at one point in time was the type of study design selected for studies included in this book. This design requires the use of stratification and statistical controls to minimize the effect of selectivity bias which is inherent in assessing the impact of development on fertility. This bias refers to the fact that villages receiving developmental inputs are not randomly selected. Moreover, individuals benefiting from these inputs are also 'self-selected.' The effect of this bias and additional methodological issues are discussed in Chapter 7.

Level of Analysis

The level of analysis utilized in the studies included in this book can be referred to as multi-level. That is, data on variables from a higher level of aggregation are combined with data from a lower level of aggregation which allows analyses to be conducted on the relationship between the levels. For example, the studies conducted in Thailand analyze the relationship between village-level indicators of irrigation and electrification, household and individual socioeconomic characteristics and their fertility behavior. The Sri Lanka study relates household utilization of development outputs to the socioeconomic status and fertility of individuals. The remaining two studies relate socioeconomic status of individuals to individual fertility behavior.

Four of the five research studies collected village-level data and attempted a traditional ecological level of analysis of development impacts upon fertility with the village as the unit of analysis. These activities were undertaken following several workshops conducted with the researchers to identify further areas of analysis. However, the results of this analysis for all four studies proved unreliable and have not been included in the individual chapters. The reasons for this and some of the relevant results are included in Chapter 7.

Major Findings

Three of the five empirical studies included in this book focused on the impact of interventions to improve economic conditions; one in Sri Lanka and two in Thailand. The fourth focussed on the impact of female employment in industrial and non-industrial settings on fertility in the Philippines, and the fifth focussed on the impact of child labor and schooling on fertility in South India. Given the similarities of the three studies in Sri Lanka and Thailand, findings from these studies are discussed together.

Impacts of Development Projects on Fertility in Sri Lanka and Thailand

Interventions to improve economic conditions considered in the three studies included land settlement, guaranteed price scheme, rural electrification, and their combinations in Sri Lanka; and rural electrification and agricultural irrigation in Thailand.

Almost all correlation coefficients measuring the total effects of development projects upon fertility are found to be significant statistically and in the expected direction. In Sri Lanka, except for the land settlement scheme, the average current fertility (during five years prior to interview) for couples who benefited from other projects (rural electrification and the guaranteed price scheme) was lower than that of couples who did not benefit from any of the three development projects. In Thailand current fertility was lower for couples in households with electricity than for couples in households without electricity. These total effects of development projects upon fertility are hypothesized to be a function of the indirect effects of the projects upon fertility as they operate through the socioeconomic structure. If the model which tests this hypothesis is a 'valid' rendering of the relation between development and fertility, then the total of all indirect effects through various channels should be equal to or closely approximate the total effect found, i.e., the correlation coefficient. The discussion which follows focuses upon the research findings regarding the total of indirect effects obtained in the three impact studies—one in Sri Lanka and two in Thailand. The two components of these indirect effects are discussed separately. These are: the impact of development projects on the socioeconomic structure, such as occupation and income; and the impact of the socioeconomic structure on family planning and fertility. The total indirect effect of outputs of a development project on fertility is the product of these two components.

Total Indirect Effects. With the exception of irrigation projects in Thailand where the fertility effects of the project output at the village level cancelled the fertility effect of the project output at the household level, the total indirect effect of development projects upon fertility are found to be significant and negative as expected. In Sri Lanka these projects include the guaranteed price scheme alone and in combination with land settlement, and rural electrification in combination with land settlement; and in Thailand rural electrification alone. However, the indirect effects of all these projects, although significant, account for a small portion of the total effect of development on fertility.

Several possible reasons which can account for this difference are discussed in greater detail in Chapter 7. The first among these relates to the fact that some of the models utilized in the studies did not include all proximate determinants of fertility. Thus all channels through which socioeconomic structure can affect fertility cannot be specified. A second reason relates to that portion of indirect effects of development projects on fertility which might be due to an association between project outputs and other exogenous variables and therefore cannot be attributed to project outputs. The third reason relates to the time lags allowed for the effects between development and social structure, and social structure and fertility to occur. These changes are seldom short term phenomena and if sufficient time has not been allowed for them, then this would reduce the magnitudes of these effects observed in a study and would therefore minimize the contribution they make to the total indirect effect of development upon fertility. This problem has been minimized as far as possible by using measures of recent fertility and development projects which were initiated at earlier periods in time. The fourth reason relates to the fact that the model might not include all those factors which are affected by the development project outputs, on the one hand, and in turn affect the demand for children, the use of contraception and fertility.

Finally, the errors involved in the measurement of contraceptive use and fertility, and the stochastic nature of birth itself might have contributed to the low magnitude of the effect of development project outputs explained by the models. As explained in Chapter 7, the measurement of the current use of contraception as a simple dichotomous variable (i.e., using or not using) reduced the observed relationship between contraception and fertility, and between economic indicators and use of contraception. Future studies of this kind should include a better measure of contraceptive use which incorporates the duration of its use and the temporal sequence between the use and the occurrence of births during five years prior to interview. This would considerably increase the magnitude of the indirect effects of development project outputs on fertility which could be explained by the models used in these studies.

Development and Socioeconomic Structure. In general, the research projects in Sri Lanka and Thailand have demonstrated the impact of development projects upon the socioeconomic structure at the household level under different conditions existing in these countries. The magnitude of these effects, however, is higher in Sri Lanka than it is in Thailand.

The effects of the development projects on occupation and income vary by the type of project; the effect of a combination of development outputs on these economic factors is higher than the effect of the individual output; and these effects are *gender specific.* In Sri Lanka, for example, rural electrification (RE) increases participation of males in nonagricultural occupations whereas both the land settlement (LS) and guaranteed price support (GPS) projects are associated with higher participation of males in agriculture. Except for rural electrification, alone or in combination with guaranteed price support, the other four combinations of developmental outputs (GPS, LS, GPS & LS, LS & RE) increase female participation in work outside the home, including work in agriculture. All projects make a greater contribution to increasing male income than they do to increasing female income net of their education and occupation. The link between occupation and income among females is much stronger than males. An internal constraint currently affecting the level of female income in the agricultural sector is that their wage rate for the same occupation is lower than that for males.

These gender-specific impacts of development projects are the first to be empirically demonstrated in Asia. Since the Bucharest Conference, and the International Women's Year Conference of 1975, considerable attention has been directed at the issue of the relationship between women's socioeconomic status and economic development (Bossen, 1975; Mazumdar, 1977; Olin, 1980; Tinker, 1976). However, the aspect of this relationship in South and East Asia which has received little attention is the socioeconomic impacts upon women of specific development projects. The few studies conducted on impacts have focussed upon socioeconomic effects of individual development projects in a specific geographic area on very small samples of women. These include a study in Gujarat, India which found that irrigation and multiple croppings have adverse effects upon female labor force participation (Hirway, 1978); a study in peninsular Malaysia which reported that women's employment and wage rates were negatively affected by an irrigation-resettlement project (Palmer, 1979); and a study in a few villages of Northeastern Thailand which found almost no effect upon women's work roles of a rain-fed agricultural development project (Palmer *et al.*, 1983).

Thus the Sri Lanka study is the first of its type to extensively document the large-scale, gender-specific impacts of individual development projects and their combinations upon socioeconomic structure in the region.

Socioeconomic Structure and Fertility. Although development projects exert effects upon occupation and income, the effects of these socioeconomic factors upon family planning and fertility are mixed. Moreover, the magnitude of these effects is lower than that of the effects of development projects on occupation and income. For example, in Sri Lanka, participation of females in occupations outside the household does not necessarily result in a positive effect upon practice of family planning. It is the type of employment, such as participation in 'Public Sector' occupations, which is important for the increased use of contraceptives. All development projects, although they increased participation of females in occupations outside the households, did not increase their participation in 'Public Sector' occupations. However, female income appears to be more important than male income with regard to its effect on the use of contraceptives. These results suggest that those development projects which contribute to an increase in participation of females in 'Public Sector' occupations or to an increase in female income would also contribute to lower fertility.

The magnitude of the effects of occupation and income on family planning and fertility is lower than the magnitude of the effects of development projects upon occupation and income but it is not always lower than the effects of other factors such as female education on family planning and fertility. The low order of magnitude of the effects of socioeconomic factors in general may be the result of high prevalence rates of contraceptive use and the consequent lack of socioeconomic differentials in contraceptive practice. That is, when levels of prevalence reach a very high rate, for example in Thailand where the rate is over 60 percent, the differentials between socioeconomic groups are substantially reduced, which are reflected in the low values of the correlation coefficients. This contention is supported by data presented in the Thai studies.

Although Sri Lanka does not have the high rate of prevalence that Thailand has there appears to be some uniformity of contraceptive practice across income and occupation groups. A portion of this finding (see Sri Lanka study, Chapter 2) may be a result of the shift in the income distribution which occurred during political changes over the last decade which reduced inequality in the distribution, and moved couples with lower prevalence into higher income categories. In addition, the family planning program in Sri Lanka has been heavily rural-oriented with availability and accessibility of contraception widespread throughout the country. This has contributed to lower differentials in prevalence between urban and rural areas and occupational groups within the rural sector.

In conclusion, the three research studies have established that development projects do affect fertility. They have identified the statistically significant linkages within this relationship, i.e., the effect of development projects upon socioeconomic structure and the effect of the structure upon family planning and fertility, and have shown that the magnitudes of the effects reflecting the former linkages are greater than the magnitudes of the effects reflecting the latter linkages. Further, the overall effect of development outputs upon fertility were found to differ between development projects. The fertility effects of electrification are greater than the effects of irrigation projects in Thailand, and in general the combination of development projects in Sri Lanka exert greater effects upon fertility than individual development projects.

Impacts of Female Employment upon Fertility in the Philippines

Previous research on the relationship between female employment and fertility in developing countries has often failed to support the expected inverse relationship between these variables. The explanation usually proposed to account for their weak relationship is associated with the 'role incompatibility' theory. It maintains that the employment–fertility relationship should be weakest in cases where either occupational or household factors operate to reduce conflicts between working and maternal roles.

The study in the Philippines tests the applicability of the 'role incompatibility' theory in an analysis of the effects of female employment upon fertility by comparing women in three types of urban work settings with housewives. The occupational settings include a large-scale canning factory, smaller-sized shops and industries, and vendors in one of the city's four public markets.

This study also formulates and tests the validity of an explanation based upon the importance of differential breastfeeding practices. It maintains that working women are less able to nurse their newborn children, especially when they hold a job in the formal sector. Since this has the effect of contributing to the likelihood of a subsequent pregnancy, fertility differentials between employed women and housewives may thus be narrowed appreciably or even reversed.

Overall the findings failed to support the role incompatibility theory. Although fertility differentials were found among the three occupational groups they were not in the direction hypothesized by the theory. Current levels of fertility were highest among factory employees and lowest among housewives.

In contrast, the three major hypotheses postulated by the breastfeeding explanation were all confirmed. These were, first, that working women (especially factory employees) would be less likely to breastfeed their offspring than would housewives; second, that working wives, particularly those employed in the factory, would exhibit fertility levels as high as, or higher than, housewives; and, third, that controls for duration of breastfeeding should tend to reduce the magnitude of this latter relationship.

In sum, these findings have identified a major oversight of the role compatibility theory, that is, on the one hand it can create pressures toward the reduction of natality due to its hypothetically positive association with family planning use, but it can also *increase* the fertility of working women, *via* its restrictive impact upon the practice of breastfeeding. Hence, in settings where breastfeeding levels are an important factor in regulating fertility levels, either because contraception is not widely practiced or (the Philippine case) because the less effective methods are commonly employed if family planning use is fairly widespread, it is to be doubted if incompatibility between maternal and occupational roles will result in decreased fertility. This would be particularly true in situations (again, as exemplified by the Philippine case) in which breast milk substitutes are readily available, thus making viable the option of deciding not to breastfeed one's baby.

Impacts of Child Labor and Schooling on Fertility in South India

It is generally believed that fertility in developing countries is high in part (or mainly) because children make important contributions to the household in terms of both wage and non-wage work. Their schooling, on the other hand, is expected to exert downward pressure on fertility because it would reduce their contributions to the household. An alternate hypothesis is that if the children's contribution is absolutely essential for the survival of the household or if parents tend to optimize their own welfare instead of their children's, competition between children's schooling and labor input may result in high dropouts from school instead of lower fertility for parents.

The study in Karnataka State in India addressed these issues. It first established the nature and the extent of work performed by children in rural households, established a negative relationship between child labor and schooling, identified some of the important determinants of both child labor and schooling, and then studied their impacts on family planning and fertility.

On average, children in rural Karnataka spend four hours per day on work (household work and directly productive work). Their participation increases with age as expected. Sex differentials were found both in the nature of work—greater household work by girls and greater directly productive work by boys—and in the time spent on work—girls put in longer hours than boys. Relatively fewer girls than boys go to school.

A significant inverse relationship between child labor and schooling was found at the micro-level. The age of the child and the presence of younger children in the household were important predictors of child labor; and age of the child and education of the father were the important predictors for child schooling.

Although no direct relationship was found between child labor and fertility, child labor did significantly affect fertility indirectly through its negative effect upon schooling. Since schooling negatively affects fertility, the overall effect of child labor on fertility is positive. This relationship persisted net of the significant negative effects upon fertility of father's opportunity consciousness and number of living children. Further, socioeconomic factors such as landholding and father's education proved insignificant in the relationship. Hence, it would appear that both reductions in the incidence of child labor and increases in the proportions attending school and attaining higher levels of schooling will contribute to a reduction in fertility.

Related Research Activities

The fertility impact studies in this book have made important contributions to the knowledge base concerning the quantitative impact of development projects on fertility. These studies are unique because they not only assessed the impact of development projects on fertility by simple gross differences but also specified and estimated linkages through which development project outputs affect fertility. These studies found that development projects affect fertility significantly through influencing socioeconomic structure, which in turn affects the use of family planning methods. These indirect effects were found to vary between development projects. Electrification exerts a greater impact upon fertility than irrigation in Thailand, and combinations of projects exert greater impacts than individual projects in Sri Lanka. Further, the studies established empirically the gender-specific impacts of development projects upon occupation and income, and the significant indirect effects of child labor upon fertility as it operates through a decrease in time spent by children in schools in India. The Philippine study identified a major oversight of the role incompatibility theory by documenting different mechanisms through which occupational settings can influence fertility. The Indian study confirmed the expected inverse relationship between child schooling and parental fertility and showed that the effect of child labor on parental fertility is transmitted through its effect on child schooling.

These achievements must be considered in relation to efforts made under other research programs. A complete review of all this work is outside the scope of this book, but some relevant work is briefly reviewed below to illustrate their relative achievements.

The World Fertility Survey (WFS), an international program of research on human fertility throughout the world initiated in 1972, published a report on the major findings and implications of surveys conducted in forty-two developing countries and twenty developed countries (Gille, 1984). Under this program, data on community-level factors were also collected for seventeen developing countries. These data have been analyzed to study the effect of macro-level factors on micro-level behavior, which provide a broader context to the impact studies included in this book. Results of some of these analyses were presented at a conference in 1983 and are published in a volume edited by Casterline (1985a). In a review paper, Casterline (1985b; p. 14) concludes that these data 'in general failed to identify hypothesized effects of community characteristics on reproductive behavior.' The community-level and the household-level data in the WFS were not specifically designed to assess the impact of development projects on fertility. Nevertheless the results have been used to conclude that,

> On the whole WFS has not identified for policy purposes any single aspect of development that is crucial to the level of fertility decline and demographic change. Fertility decline can and does occur in widely differing socio-economic contexts. Its onset appears to be determined more by ill-understood cultural factors than by any objectively ascertainable development factors. [Gille, 1984, p. 40.]

An International Consortium of Population Research Centers established with funds from the UNFPA and the Rockefeller Foundation has been involved in five studies concerned with the population impact of rural development projects in the Philippines, Thailand, Nigeria, Brazil and Colombia. The results from these studies are published in a volume edited by Bilsborrow and Delargy (1985). None of the five case studies, according to the editors, 'has strong enough findings to base broad policies on at this point, but they do give clues to problem areas which should be investigated further and to the additional kinds of information which should be collected,' (p. 192). A number of reasons contributed to this type of conclusion. For example, the projects were not comparable, all projects did not include the same parameters, and 'none of the five case study authors documented the *economic* effects of their projects,' (p. 190).

Another volume consisting of five case studies on the demographic impact of Asian development projects was edited by Barlow (1982). These case studies focussed primarily on the development of methodologies to estimate the potential demographic impacts of development projects. One of the studies, however, used existing data from the Comilla project in Bangladesh, and concluded that the project probably had little effect on fertility. This study and two other studies included in this volume, however, demonstrated the antinatalist influence of social aspects of development such as female education and family planning.

An ILO report reviewed the experience of various organizations until 1984 concerning the integration of population in development planning. All agencies reviewed in this report have had only limited success with planning bodies in convincing them to incorporate population concerns in development planning. General conclusions emphasize a weak conceptual base, crude measurement techniques, and lack of operational advice to planners after ten years of effort. Not surprisingly, one of the recommendations concerns the improvement in quantitative methodologies designed to assess the way in which various socioeconomic factors and government interventions affect fertility, mortality and migration (ILO, 1984).

Two other efforts should also be mentioned, both of which provide exhaustive reviews of the literature concerning relationships between fertility and its determinants. Neither one of them contains empirical information about the effect of development projects on fertility.

One of these includes an extensive review of the existing knowledge concerning the determinants of fertility in developing countries. This review, conducted under the auspices of the Panel on Fertility Determinants of the Committee on Population and Demography of the National Research Council, has been published in two volumes edited by Bulatao and Lee (1983). The editors in the overview chapter mention that,

> the current fertility situation of the developing countries is a complex of interrelated factors. From this perspective, the debate about whether development or family planning is primarily responsible for lowering fertility is largely beside the point; both are integral parts of an intricate process that no two countries pass through in exactly the same manner. [Bulatao & Lee, 1983, pp. 785–6.]

The second effort refers to a book edited by Schutjer and Stokes (1984), which includes review chapters on the relationships between fertility and one of the several determinants—female employment, income, income distribution, the value of children, nutrition, etc. The review of the literature about these links is exhaustive but, as mentioned by Simmons (1984) in the last chapter on Conclusions and Policy Implications, '[it] reveals the deficiencies of the existing knowledge base in attempts to predict the fertility effects of these development factors,' (p. 295). This volume, although it discussed a number of policy issues and implications of existing knowledge base to design 'fertility-sensitive rural development policy,' does not include any empirical study which either documents the effect of any specific development project on fertility or estimates the linkages between project outputs and fertility behavior.

Implications for Further Research

The purpose of the fertility impact studies is to quantify the actual fertility changes (differences) attributable to inputs provided through development projects. These research efforts are basically geared to identify points of interventions which will affect demographic processes in the long run. Each link in the chain of events between the initiation of a development project and its ultimate effect on fertility requires time: time for the initial study to measure the effect of development projects on fertility; for translating and disseminating the policy relevance of the research findings to policymakers; for changes in the allocation of resources to take place assuming that fertility impacts are taken into consideration; and for the implementation of these policy changes to have some measurable impact on fertility. A quick glance will be sufficient to indicate that this is a long-term process. These issues of time lags must be clearly understood so that expectations are not raised regarding short-term solutions. Since the population problems are not short term in nature, these types of research efforts are important because they are most likely to have a significant effect on the demographic processes in the long run (see Jain, 1978, for further discussion of the utility of research on the demographic impacts of development).

In order to enhance the utilization of these activities, researchers need to understand the process of decision-making, and need to identify various elements and their relative importance that are considered by policymakers in selecting a particular strategy. This can best be done by establishing active collaboration between researchers and those responsible for selecting, designing, and implementing development programs at various stages, from the formulation of a research problem to the implementation of its findings.

The utility of fertility impact studies can be further enhanced by monitoring changes associated with new development projects right from the beginning rather than trying to estimate change attributable to these projects after their completion. The projects for this purpose, however, should be carefully selected. First priority should be assigned to those projects which are organized to directly affect people in the project area; designed to influence those social, economic, and cultural conditions that are believed to affect fertility by reducing childbearing incentives and increasing the cost of childbearing; organized at the subnational, well-defined geographic area with a population of about 50,000; and have some evaluation plan to study the effect of project outputs on socioeconomic structure in the project area.

Although prospective studies are expensive and difficult to carry out, we believe such studies can be much more useful than the cross-sectional type of studies. The outcome of such studies can be further improved if they are conducted in areas with a good vital registration system.

In areas with poor registration systems, good surrogate indexes need to be developed to measure the impact of development projects on fertility. These indexes might include such factors as costs and benefits of children, familial institutions, preferred or desired family size. Other indexes may include such key factors as *infant and child mortality*, *child labor and schooling*, *female education*, and *women's income and employment*, which are usually found to be associated with a demand for smaller families and an increase in the use of contraception. Research on project-specific impact on and determinants of these known or presumed key determinants of fertility would help to identify ways to modify them through development policies and programs in a way that potential changes in these determinants are consistent with demographic objectives.

Implications for Population Policy

A number of implications for population policy can be drawn from the studies included in this book. First, it has been demonstrated for electrification and guaranteed price support projects and combinations of projects, for example, guaranteed price support with land settlement or electrification, that their effects upon fertility are greater than land settlement alone or in combination with electrification projects. These effects operate through the socioeconomic structure and the practice of family planning. Hence, it could be inferred that the antinatalistic effects of development could be maximized by a policy of spreading rural electrification and implementing guaranteed price support schemes alone or in combination with electrification or land settlement projects in areas where family planning services are already available and accessible. A corollary of this finding is that the land settlement schemes without some of the other support systems (family planning services, rural electrification, guaranteed minimum price for the products) is likely to increase fertility. Therefore, in designing land settlement schemes, adequate attention should be paid to provide other support systems.

Second, attention should be given to the *type* of female employment generated by current and future development projects. As several of the impact studies found, it is not sufficient for development projects to create female employment outside of the home to affect fertility. It is the *type* of employment that is crucial for income generation and increase in contraceptive use and ultimately to decrease fertility. Therefore, policies directed at increasing female employment in the 'appropriate' types of occupations (e.g., non-agricultural and public sector) within current and future development projects could result in greater antinatalistic impacts of these projects.

Third, the findings have provided the basis for a policy recommendation that may contribute to a reduction in fertility that does not require changes in project designs or the existing social structure. In Sri Lanka the gender specific impacts of development upon occupation and the relationship between female occupation and income and family planning indicate that if female income were raised within the existing occupational structure, it would contribute to an increase in contraceptive practice and a decrease in fertility. Since there is currently an inequality in wage rates between females and males within the same occupations in the agricultural sector, a policy directed at reducing this inequality could contribute to lower fertility. A policy of this nature would of course have to take into account the possible restriction in the employment of females which might follow its implementation.

Fourth, findings from the Philippine study indicate that reduced breastfeeding resulting from the structure of the work setting is the primary factor explaining the absence of expected fertility differentials between different occupational groups, and between these groups and housewives. The authors maintain that to achieve a reduction in fertility, policies will be necessary to alter the structure of the work setting for females. These policies would include government subsidized day care centers and nurseries and/or company based child care facilities. This latter policy could be incorporated within a larger program of maternity benefits which would also provide periodic work breaks for females for the purpose of breastfeeding.

Fifth, the Indian study found that child labor increased parental fertility indirectly by decreasing the time children spent in schools. Child schooling, on the other hand, was found to exert a significant negative effect upon parental fertility. Hence, policies directed at reducing the requirements for child labor and increasing the chances of children to enroll and remain in school would be expected to contribute to a reduction in fertility.

The authors of the India study have pointed out that a policy which would compensate families for their children's labor would be very expensive; however, a more practical alternative would be to eliminate the need for some of the work done by children. In the Indian context a large portion of the work of children consists of tending cattle and doing routine household chores such as fetching water from a well or a river, grinding spices, cleaning and washing of foodgrains and vegetables for cooking, and fetching firewood. The authors of the India study suggest that a policy which would provide better water and fuel facilities for villages, clean and ready to cook foodgrains, and arrangements for communal tending of cattle could make a contribution to a reduction in the need for children's labor and allow them time to attend school. This policy would compensate parents indirectly for child labor but, since it might involve major infrastructure costs, it is not clear whether these policies will be more cost-effective than the direct compensation. In addition, direct policies to improve schooling facilities for girls would increase their enrolment and would ultimately contribute to a reduction in fertility through the resulting higher rates of contraception among parents.

Sixth, given the rather robust association generally found between female education and fertility, a policy which would reduce the school drop-out rate for females in particular might be expected to have the maximum antinatalistic effect. This would be the case because the higher levels of educational attainment reached would also be expected to affect their fertility when they go through their reproductive period.

Finally, the impact of development projects on fertility can also be enhanced by incorporating the information about the use of family planning at the time of designing these projects. This can be achieved in two ways: (a) by including the extent of contraceptive use among the criteria for selecting geographic areas to be covered by a development project, and (b) by ensuring that the information and services for family planning methods are made available in geographic units selected for a development project.

Following the Bucharest Conference, unrealistic expectations were created regarding the role of development in reducing fertility. As such, a number of efforts were made to identify a single dimension intervention as an alternative to family planning. As the brief review of some of these efforts, presented earlier, suggests, there is no single path from high to low fertility. If so, the effects of governmental interventions on fertility must be viewed as additive. Since governments will continue to design and implement development policies and programs, efforts must be made to enhance the fertility reduction effect of all appropriate interventions. The fertility impact studies can make important contributions in this respect. The results of these studies are unlikely to be useful in rejecting a particular project because most of the development programs can be adequately justified on the basis of their primary objectives alone. The outcome of these studies, as shown previously, can generate guidelines to assign higher priority to some types of development efforts on the basis of their potential antinatalistic effects. They can also be useful in improving the design of a particular project in order to enhance its antinatalistic effect.

References

Barlow, Robin (ed.), 1982. *Case Study in the Demographic Impact of Asian Development Projects*. Ann Arbor, Michigan, Center for Research on Economic Development, University of Michigan.

Bilsborrow, Richard E., & Pamela F. Delargy (eds.), 1985. *Impact of Rural Development Projects on Demographic Behavior*. Population Studies No.9, New York, United Nations Fund for Population Activities.

Bongaarts, John, 1978. 'A Framework for Analyzing the Proximate Determinants of Fertility.' *Population and Development Review* **4** (1), pp.105–32.

Bossen, Laurel, 1975. 'Women in Modernizing Societies.' *American Ethnologist*, **2**, No. 6, 587–601.

Bulatao, Rodolfo A., & Lee, Ronald D. (eds.) with Paula E. Hollerbach and John Bongaarts. 1983. *Determinants of Fertility in Developing Countries: A Summary of Knowledge*. Vols. 1 and 2, New York, Academic Press.

Casterline, John B. (ed.), 1985a. *The Collection and Analysis of Community Data*. Voorburg, Netherlands, International Statistical Institute.

Casterline, John B., 1985b. 'The Macro Determinants of Fertility: Lessons from the WFS Experience.' Paper presented at the 1985 Annual Meeting of the Population Association of America, Boston.

Coale, Ansley J., and Hoover, Edgar M. 1958. *Population Growth and Economic Development in Low-Income Countries*. Princeton, Princeton University Press.

Cutright, Phillips, 1983. 'The Ingredients of Recent Fertility Decline in Developing Countries,' *International Family Planning Perspectives* **9** (4), pp.101–9.

Davis, Kingsley & Blake, Judith, 1956. 'Social Structure and Fertility: An Analytical Framework.' *Economic Development and Cultural Change* **4** (4), pp.211–35.

Gille, Halvor, 1984. *World Fertility Survey: Major Findings and Implications*. Voorburg, International Statistical Institute.

Hirway, Indira, 1978. 'Irrigation and Women's Work in Gujarat,' paper presented at Seminar on 'Women as Partners in Progress.' New Delhi, India.

International Labour Office, 1984. *Report of the Informal Inter-Agency Expert Group Meeting on Methodologies for Integrated Population and Development Planning*. Geneva, International Labour Office.

Jain, Anrudh K., 1978. 'Some Issues Pertinent to the Assessment of Demographic Impacts of Development Policies.' *Working Paper No. 1*, International Programs, The Population Council, New York.

Mauldin, W. Parker, & Lapham, Robert J. , 1984. 'Conditions of Fertility Decline in LDCs: 1965–1980.' Paper presented at the 1984 annual meeting of the Population Association of America.

Mazumdar, Vina (ed.), 1977. *Role of Rural Women in Development*, report of an International Study Seminar held at the Institute of Development Studies, University of Sussex (Bombay, Delhi, and Calcutta, Allied Publishers Private, Ltd.).

Miro, Carmen A., & Potter, Joseph E., 1980. *Population Policy: Research Priorities in the Developing World*. London, Frances Pinter (Publishers).

McNicoll, Geoffrey, 1984. 'Consequences of Rapid Population Growth: An Overview and Assessment.' *Population and Development Review*, **10** (2), pp.177–240.

National Research Council, 1986. *Population Growth and Economic Development: Policy Questions*. Washington, D.C., National Academy Press.

Olin, Ulla, 1980. *Rural Women's Participation in Development*. Evaluation Study No. 3, New York, United Nations Development Program.

Palmer, Ingrid, 1979. *The Nemow Case*. International Programs Working Paper No. 7, The Population Council, New York.

Palmer, Ingrid, Subhadhira, Sukaesinee and Grisanaputi, Wilaiwat, 1983. *Northeast Rainfed Agricultural Development Project in Thailand: A Baseline Survey of Women's Roles and Household Resource Allocation for a Farming Systems Approach*. Study No. 3, International Programs, The Population Council, New York.

Schutjer, Wayne A., & Stokes, C. Shannon (eds.), 1984. *Rural Development and Human Fertility*. New York, Macmillan.

Simmons, Ozzie G., 1984. 'Conclusions and Policy Implications,' in W. A. Schutjer and C. S. Stokes (eds.), *Rural Development and Human Fertility*. New York, Macmillan.

Tinker, Irene, (ed.), 1976. *Women and World Development*. Washington, DC, Overseas Development Council.

United Nations, 1985. *Proceedings of the United Nations Ad Hoc Expert Group Meeting on the Manual on Integrating Population Variables Into Development Planning*. New York, United Nations (ESA/P/WP/87).

2 Fertility Impacts of Development Programs in Sri Lanka

*N. L. Sirisena and John Stoeckel**

Introduction

The Problem and Objectives

During the past four decades development programs implemented in Sri Lanka have included: land settlement schemes which utilize irrigation; guaranteed price schemes which develop markets for agricultural produce; and rural electrification. To date, no systematic attempt has been made to assess the (individual or collective) impact of one or more of these programs either upon the social and economic structure of the country or upon fertility. Previous studies have focussed on establishing fertility differentials with respect to household and individual characteristics such as male and female education, work status, occupation, standard of living, ethnicity, type of place and region of residence (see, for example, Fernando, 1974; Hanna & Madarajah, 1976; Kumaraswamy, 1956; Langford, 1981; Little & Perera, 1981; Raja, 1954; and Sarkar, 1954). The objective of this study is to analyze the effect of development programs on socioeconomic structure, and on fertility. This will be done by comparing couples who benefited from a number of development program inputs with those who lived in villages which did not receive any of the development inputs under consideration. Before proceeding with the detailed explanation of how the objective of this study will be attained, a brief overview of the demographic background of the country and development programs is presented.

*N. L. Sirisena is with The Statistics Branch, Central Bank of Sri Lanka and John Stoeckel is with The Population Council.

Demographic Background

The growth of population in Sri Lanka during the last hundred years has not been uniform. Until 1946 the average annual intercensal rate of growth never exceeded 2 percent, and generally fluctuated between 0.9 percent and 1.7 percent. However, during the years following World War II, the annual rate of population growth increased sharply from about 1.5 percent in 1946 to over 2.7 percent in the early 1960s. The rapid increase was brought about by a dramatic decline in the death-rate. While the birth-rate fluctuated between 35 to 40 per thousand, the death rate declined from around 20 per thousand in 1946 to slightly over 14 in 1947, as a result of an intensive DDT spraying campaign for the eradication of malaria. By the end of 1962 the death-rate had dropped further, to about 10 (Department of Census and Statistics, 1974).

During the remainder of the 1960s the birth-rate declined to around 32 while the death rate reached 8, resulting in an annual growth rate of about 2.4 percent. From 1970 to the end of the decade the birth-rate declined steadily, to around 27, and the death-rate dropped to about 7. This resulted in a growth rate of about 2 percent per year for the country's population of approximately 15 million in 1980.

Development Programs

Guaranteed Price Scheme (GPS). The GPS, initiated in 1948, was a voluntary purchasing scheme for rice-producing farmers aimed at improving the open market price for paddy by providing price guarantees (for paddy) and a lower selling price for fertilizer and seeds. Generally, four stages have characterized the evolution of the scheme. In the first, between 1948 and 1956, the scheme had difficulty in competing with private traders who could provide credit to the paddy producer. As a result, the GPS could only collect a small share of the market surplus of paddy directly from the paddy producer. However, since the scheme offered a price higher than the open market, the government did collect a substantial portion of the paddy produced in the country by purchasing it from the private traders.

During the second stage, 1956–71, the purchasing power of the scheme increased dramatically—through an arrangement with the cooperative movement and the banking system. The system provided credit facilities to cooperatives for the GPS purchases under a special credit arrangement with the Central Bank, which financed loans to cooperatives at a concessionary interest rate of 3 percent. At this point the cooperatives began selling fertilizer and high-yielding seed varieties to farmers on credit in addition to purchasing paddy. By 1970 GPS purchases of paddy reached 26 million bushels, which accounted for over a third of the country's total production; and provided subsidies to farmers of over 177 million rupees (GSL, 1970).

In the third stage, 1972–6, the Paddy Marketing Board (PMB) was created to act as a sole implementor of the GPS; and was given, among other powers, a monopoly for purchasing paddy by the Paddy Marketing Act of 1971. This changed the approach of the GPS from market promotion and competition to one of restricting competition. One of the factors responsible for this change was the financial problem associated with implementing the government food policy of obtaining rice for distribution under a good ration scheme. Although the GPS was to be utilized to purchase rice for the ration scheme, the cost of imported rice was actually lower than the cost of locally produced rice. Since the government responded by raising imports, local paddy output declined slightly during the period. Although the subsidies paid to paddy producers reached over 250 million rupees, GPS purchases of paddy were down slightly to 24.5 million bushels, which accounted for about 21 percent of total production (GSL, 1981).

In 1977, the beginning of the fourth stage, the restrictions on paddy marketing were removed and the PMB no longer maintained its monopoly. During the next three years the paddy sector expanded 10 percent annually and the purchases by the PMB increased accordingly. However, since 1980 the purchases by the PMB declined as private traders began to offer more attractive prices to producers. Hence, the GPS has evolved into a 'floor price scheme' with the PMB playing the role of a 'floor price' operator, intervening in the paddy market when prices are lower, particularly during post-harvest periods (CBC, 1981).

The GPS created a major transformation in the paddy sector, i.e. from a subsistence orientation to a production and market orientation. Specific aspects of the scheme contributing to this transformation included the provision of credit, the availability and use of fertilizer, high-yielding seed varieties, agro-chemicals, and the adoption of more productive agricultural practices.

Land Settlement (LS) Scheme. A number of LS schemes, all of which are characterized by some type of irrigation, have been implemented in Sri Lanka since the early 1950s. The first scheme, which is still one of the largest in the country, is Gal Oya, with over 26,000 families settled. Under this scheme, initiated in 1952, house construction and land development were completed prior to the settlers' arrival. Each family was given five acres of land for paddy cultivation and three acres for a home garden. The total land area under paddy cultivation was approximately 130,000 acres (GSL, 1979).

During the latter part of the 1950s, two small schemes, the Mapakada and Dambarawa, were implemented. Land allotments per family were generally about one acre, with a total land area under paddy cultivation of approximately 2,500 acres.

In the late 1960s a new policy referred to as 'advanced settlement' was utilized by the government in two LS schemes, the Uda Walawe and Rajangana. Under this policy settlers were paid a subsistence allowance (lower than average wages) and were responsible for the construction of their own housing. In the Uda Walawe scheme each family received 3 acres for paddy cultivation and 2 acres for a home garden. Approximately 14,000 families participate in this scheme, with a land area under paddy cultivation of about 40,000 acres (GSL, 1979, p.84).

In the Rajangana scheme the cultivation of subsidiary food crops in addition to paddy cultivation was facilitated by the introduction of lift irrigation for the highland areas. Families settling in these areas were given one-acre plots for subsidiary crop cultivation and half an acre for a home garden; those in the lowland areas received 2 acres for paddy cultivation and half an acre for a home garden. Over ten thousand families were settled in the two areas, with about 16,000 acres utilized for the cultivation of crops other than paddy (GSL, 1979, p. 102).

In 1970 the multi-purpose Mahaweli project was initiated. This project, originally planned for completion in thirty years (efforts are being made by the government to reduce the time period), will benefit a large portion of the country's 'Dry Zone' through irrigation and the production of 500 megawatts of electricity. Each family under the project will receive between 2 acres and half an acre for cultivation and half an acre for home garden. It is expected that over half a million people will be settled by the project, which would result in a total population of settlers under the LS scheme at over 1.5 million (GSL, 1982).

Rural Electrification (RE). During the 1950s and 1960s electricity was primarily generated in urban areas from a hydro-electric plant at the upper reaches of the Kelani ganga. By the end of the 1960s multi-purpose river development programs began to be implemented to supply electricity to the rural areas. From 1968 to 1970, eighty-seven RE schemes were created, while between 1970 and 1977 another 836 were implemented. Over half of the schemes were established in just six districts. These districts and their current percentage of households with electricity are as follows: Colombo—49 percent; Gampaha—45 percent; Galle and Matara—34 percent; and Ratanapura and Kulutara—32 percent. Until the completion of the Mahaweli project, almost half of rural households will continue to be without electricity (GSL, 1980).

Conceptual Framework

The conceptual framework utilized for the study at the household and individual level is shown in Figure 2.1. In general, the impact of development programs on fertility is viewed as an indirect one, operating through changes in socioeconomic status which affect fertility through changes in demand for children and the intermediate variables. The working hypothesis generated from this framework is as follows: utilization of development program outputs will exert an influence upon occupational status and income which will affect fertility through changes in the intermediate variables. The rationale for this hypothesis is discussed for each of the development programs below.

Guaranteed Price Scheme (GPS). Paddy production in Sri Lanka increased by about 90 percent between 1950 and 1979, and yield per acre improvement was a major contribution towards this increase (Department of Census and Statistics, 1981). The GPS is considered to be one of the primary factors responsible for the yield increase through the financial incentives and actual remuneration provided to farmers. This allowed farmers to sell their surplus paddy for prices higher than the open market price and in turn purchase fertilizers, agro-chemicals and high yielding seed varieties which contributed to increased production and farm income. The increase

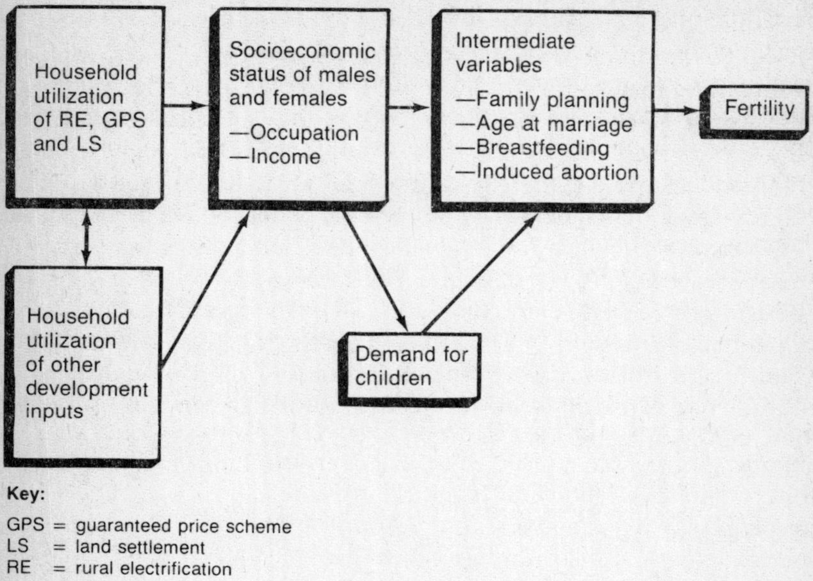

Figure 2.1 Conceptual framework for the interrelationship between development program outputs and fertility.

in income is expected to affect fertility decisions, reduce the demand for children, and lower actual fertility through an increase in the use of family planning.

Land Settlement (LS) Scheme. The acquisition of land is expected to alter labor utilization within the household and provide greater opportunities for females to participate in agricultural occupations outside the household. The allotment of land per family requires that family members contribute to the working of the land; however, because of the size of allotment, outside labor is often used to supplement the labor of family members. This allows the adoption of more intensive cultivation practices such as transplanting and row seeding and ultimately to increased agricultural production and income.

The irrigation component of the LS program contributes to a more effective land use pattern, higher cropping intensity and increased farm production, which also results in higher farm incomes. This increase in income, together with increased female labor force participation, which alters the time allocation of women within households, is expected to decrease the demand for children, resulting in higher practice of family planning and lower fertility. *Rural Electrification (RE).* The availability of electricity contributes to the establishment of new agro-centered industries and generates opportunities for employment in both farm and non-farm type occupations which may enable females to participate in production. The new types of employment particularly for females should create alternative occupational roles for them and lead ultimately to an improvement in their social status. This is expected to affect women's allocation of time within households, making less time available for raising children. This factor, in addition to the less labor-intensive methods of production made possible by electrification, for example pump extraction of water as opposed to manually obtaining and hauling water by children, reduces the utility of children for their labor. The expected increase in household income coupled with these factors would result in decreased demand for children, lower family size norms, higher practice of family planning and lower fertility.

Methodology

Sample Design

A multi-stage stratified sampling design was utilized for the study. In the first stage a listing of Government Agents (GA) Divisions were divided into seven strata according to the program inputs: GPS, LS, RE, their mixes—GPS & RE, LS & GPS, RE & LS—and where no development programs (NDP) existed. A random sample of GA divisions was selected from each of these strata. In the second stage a random sample of Grama Sevaka (GS) Divisions was selected from the GA divisions of each stratum. The third stage consisted of a random selection of census blocks (villages) from the GA divisions of each stratum. In the fourth stage a listing of all households in each census block was prepared and a 50 percent random sample of households was selected. All currently married females aged 15–44 years in those households which actually utilized or participated in a development program were included for interview. The participation in a development program was defined as those households which were registered with the government as suppliers of paddy under the guaranteed price scheme; those households which were resettled and received land under the land settlement scheme; and those households which received electricity under the rural electrification program. In the NDP census blocks of married females from the entire 50 percent sample were interviewed. A summary of the sample design and proportions of units selected at the different stages is presented in Table 2.1.

Table 2.1 Summary of stages in sample design

Programs	Stage 1	Stage 2	Stage 3	Stage 4
	No. of GA Divisions	Percent GS Divivsions selected	Percent census blocks selected	No. of households
NDP	33	1.8	6.8	687
GPS	17	2.0	8.3	575
LS	29	1.6	6.7	561
RE	25	1.3	8.2	232
GPS & RE	13	2.6	7.0	512
LS & GPS	17	2.6	9.3	544
RE & LS	17	4.8	6.7	486

Data Collection

Extreme care was taken to insure that the most reliable data possible were collected. The ratio of interviewers to supervisors was five to one and each supervisor was responsible to a senior project staff member. All interviews were checked in the field by the supervisors and staff. A 10 percent re-interview of the total sample conducted by the supervisors found a consistency of response of about 96 percent with the original interview.

Analytical Framework

The operational definitions of the variables included in the analysis are as follows:

1. development program outputs—the household utilization of and participation in GPS, RE, LS, GPS & RE, RE & LS and LS & GPS programs;
2. socioeconomic status
   a) males—employment in non-agricultural occupations, average monthly income, and number of years of formal education;
   b) females—employment in non-household occupations, average monthly income, and number of years of formal education;
3. family planning practice—use of contraception (excluding traditional methods) in the year prior to survey;
4. fertility—number of live births during five years prior to survey.

Village-level development indicators that were considered for inclusion in the analysis in addition to the development programs were: number of schools, number of family planning clinics, distance to clinics, and size of LS schemes. However, analysis of variance with the endogenous variables, fertility, family planning, occupation and income, indicated no significant relationships. Similarly, household measures of length of time of use of electricity, and years of participation in GPS showed no significant relationship with the endogenous variables.

The measure of recent fertility was selected to maximize as far as possible the time between the implementation of the development programs and the occurrence of fertility. The dates of implementation for each of the programs are as follows: GPS—1948 to 1969; LS—1952 to 1968; RE—1969 to 1977. Since fertility in the present survey is for the period 1977–81 the implementation of the development programs generally occurred a substantial number of years prior to fertility.

Path analysis was utilized to estimate the effects of development program outputs on fertility transmitted through socioeconomic characteristics of males and females and the use of contraception. This technique was applied to models for each development program and their mixes (six program regimes) and for males and females (married five years and longer) separately. In all, twelve models have been utilized. The effect of one or more development program outputs on socioeconomic status was estimated by comparing households benefiting from the specific program outputs with those selected from areas which received no development inputs. OLS regression of each endogenous variable upon the factors which directly affect them was utilized since this method produces the lowest standard errors of the estimated coefficients (Goldberger, 1970). The general model and equations for solution of the model are as shown in Figure 2.2.

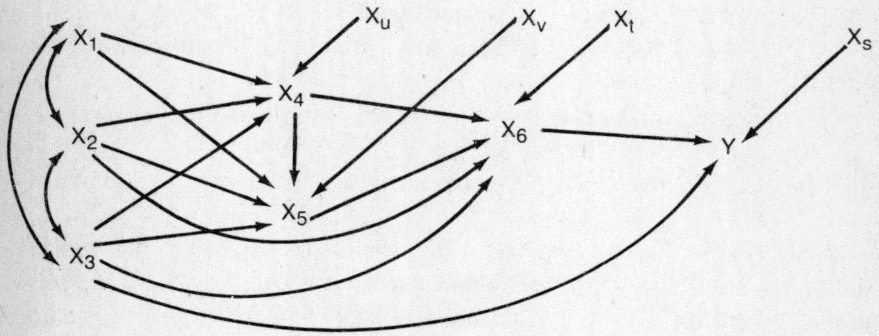

$Y = p_{o6} X_6 + p_{o3} X_3 + p_{os} X_s$
$X_6 = p_{65} X_5 + p_{64} X_4 + p_{63} X_3 + p_{62} X_2 + p_{6t} X_t$
$X_5 = p_{54} X_4 + p_{53} X_3 + p_{52} X_2 + p_{51} X_1 + p_{5v} X_v$
$X_4 = p_{43} X_3 + p_{42} X_2 + p_{41} X_1 + p_{4u} X_u$

where Y = fertility; X_6 = family planning practice; X_5 = income; X_4 = occupation; X_3 = marital duration; X_2 = educational attainment; and X_1 = LS & GPS development program output.

Figure 2.2 Model showing the effect of development program outputs on fertility.

Results and Discussion

As posited in the conceptual framework, the impact of development programs upon fertility is necessarily indirect, operating through changes in socioeconomic status which affect the intermediate variables. The following analysis is organized into two sections intended to reflect this framework. In the first section we analyze the impact of development programs upon the socioeconomic status of males and females separately, using multiple regression; and in the second section we utilize path analysis to illustrate the relationships and linkages between development programs, socioeconomic status, family planning and fertility. The rationale for organizing the first section separately from the second is that while a considerable amount of research conducted in the past has demonstrated the effect of socioeconomic status on fertility, relationships, no research has been conducted to measure the differential impacts of development programs on socioeconomic status. Without a demonstration of this latter relationship it would make little sense to measure the impact of development on fertility since this effect must operate through socioeconomic status.

Impacts of Development Programs on Socioeconomic Status

Table 2.2 presents the results of the multiple regression analyses to show the effects of individual development programs and their mixes on male non-agricultural occupations, female non-household occupations, and male and female income after controlling for the effects of male and female educational attainment. In these regressions the reference point for individual programs and their mixes is the households selected from areas receiving no development program input.

Male Occupation. The participation of males in non-agricultural occupations increases with their education. In comparison, all of the development programs and their mixes exhibit a significant negative effect net of educational attainment upon participation of males in non-agricultural occupations. However, RE is the only program whose effect is positive, which is consistent with the expectation that electrification should contribute to the creation of employment in new small-scale industries and businesses. Cross tabulations (See Table 2.3) between occupations and development programs indicate that about half the males in households with electricity are employed in 'manufacturing and commercial' occupations, while a third are employed in the 'public sector'. These latter occupations include government service as well as government-owned corporations.

Table 2.2 Standardized regression coefficients (betas) for male and female occupation and income regressed on development programs and other selected variables in Sri Lanka, 1982

Independent variables*	Non-agricultural occupation	Non-household occupation	Income	
	Male	Female	Male	Female
GPS	-0.38**	0.44**	0.39**	0.01
Education	0.08**	-0.17**	0.36**	0.07**
Occupation			-0.04	0.77**
R^2 =	0.15	0.22	0.31	0.59
(N = 1,041)				
LS	-0.47**	0.28**	0.32**	0.04**
Education	0.08	-0.16**	0.29**	0.04**
Occupation			-0.03	0.86**
R^2 =	0.23	0.11	0.18	0.75
(N = 1,037)				
RE	0.28**	0.04	0.21**	0.13**
Education	0.18**	-0.19**	0.40**	0.10**
Occupation			0.10**	0.83**
R^2 =	0.15	0.03	0.31	0.68**
(N = 768)				
GPS + RE	-0.08**	0.06†	0.63**	0.15**
Education	0.14**	-0.18	0.30**	0.09**
Occupation			-0.07**	0.72**
R^2 =	0.02	0.03	0.57	0.54
(N = 975)				
LS + GPS	-0.47**	0.41**	0.24**	0.06**
Education	0.02	-0.20**	0.28**	-0.02
Occupation			-0.05**	0.81**
R^2 =	0.22	0.22	0.15	0.69
(N = 985)				
RE + LS	-0.35**	0.46**	0.62**	0.13**
Education	0.16**	-0.14**	0.24**	0.06**
Occupation			-0.07**	0.67**
R^2 =	0.12	0.21	0.54	0.54
(N = 969)				

* Male education is used in the regressions for male income and occupation; female education is used in regressions for female occupation and income; and male and female occupation are used in regressions for male and female income, respectively. All the beta coefficients shown in this table are also adjusted for the effect of the life cycle variable—duration of marriage.

**$p < 0.001$

† $p < 0.01$

Among the programs that decrease male participation in non-agricultural occupations, the most important predictors are the LS program and the combined LS and GPS programs, which are followed by GPS and RE & LS. The GPS & RE program is the least important predictor and is the only program where education is a more important predictor of male non-agricultural occupation.

Male Income. The development programs and their mixes all show a significant positive relationship with male income. The programs with the highest predictive value are RE in combination with GPS and LS. RE & LS is about three times more important than education in predicting income, while GPS & RE is more than twice as important as education. Both the programs are nine times more important than occupation in predicting income.

It should be emphasized here that although RE alone ranks the lowest among the predictors it is the combination of RE with the other two programs which exerts the greatest influence on income. This suggests that electrification is a crucial component to effectively raise income through agriculturally based development programs such as land settlement and guaranteed price schemes. Electrification is particularly important in the former program which includes agricultural irrigation systems. The provision of electricity would be expected to make these systems cheaper and more efficient in pumping water from rivers, canals, tube wells and open wells. The end result would be higher agricultural production through higher crop yields which would ultimately raise farm income.

The presence of electrification with both development programs could also contribute to more efficient rice production through the utilization of electric rice mills. In addition, electrification contributes to the growth of agro-processing industries by making available refrigeration for storage of produce, for example fruit and vegetables. Hence, a more improved land use pattern becomes possible with greater crop diversification and increased output which would contribute to higher income.

Female Occupation. The participation of females in non-household occupations decreases with an increase in their education. In comparison, all development programs (except RE) exert a positive effect on female occupation. Three of these programs, RE & LS, GPS, and LS & GPS, are of almost equally high importance in predicting participation of females in non-household occupations. RE & LS is over three times as important as education in predicting

Table 2.3 Male and female occupation, income and education distribution (in %) by development programs

Variables	Development programs						NDP
	RE	GPS	LS	GPS&RE	LS&GPS	RE&LS	
Male occupation							
Agriculture	8.9	85.7	85.2	53.8	81.5	75.4	51.7
Cottage industries	0.8	1.2	2.9	–	–	1.2	1.0
Manufacturing and Commercial	49.4	1.4	5.1	21.6	0.8	8.6	25.1
Public sector	33.0	10.1	5.7	17.0	7.1	14.0	12.7
Unemployed	7.9	1.6	1.1	7.6	10.6	0.8	9.5
Total	100	100	100	100	100	100	100
N =	(195)	(469)	(464)	(404)	(412)	(396)	(573)
Female occupation							
Agriculture	–	63.4	49.2	13.1	64.2	57.8	16.0
Cottage industries	2.2	–	0.2	0.2	–	–	–
Manufacturing and Commercial	3.4	–	1.3	–	–	–	5.7
Public sector	10.8	1.4	0.7	8.6	1.5	6.6	0.7
Household	83.6	35.2	48.6	78.1	34.3	35.6	77.6
Total	100	100	100	100	100	100	100
N =	(195)	(469)	(464)	(404)	(412)	(396)	(573)
Male income							
None	5.6	9.0	5.9	7.0	10.0	4.5	8.9
<500 Rs.	29.9	16.8	29.5	3.2	32.8	3.9	65.8
501–800 Rs.	33.8	44.6	45.9	18.2	38.8	23.2	19.4
801–1,100 Rs.	21.0	19.4	17.0	19.4	11.2	23.5	4.9
1100 + Rs.	9.7	10.2	1.7	52.2	7.3	44.9	1.0
Total	100	100	100	100	100	100	100
N =	(195)	(469)	(464)	(404)	(412)	(396)	(573)
Female income							
None	79.5	27.3	48.1	72.3	26.7	26.8	75.6
<500 Rs.	7.7	65.9	47.6	13.6	65.3	57.2	23.8
501–800 Rs.	7.2	3.6	3.9	7.7	7.0	8.6	0.2
801–1,100 Rs.	5.6	2.8	0.2	5.2	0.5	5.6	0.2
1100 + Rs.	0.0	0.4	0.2	1.2	0.5	1.8	0.2
Total	100	100	100	100	100	100	100
N =	(195)	(469)	(464)	(404)	(412)	(396)	(573)

Table 2.3 (cont.)

Variables	Development programs						NDP
	RE	GPS	LS	GPS&RE	LS&GPS	RE&LS	
Male education							
None	4.7	12.7	12.9	8.6	14.7	6.6	18.3
1–6 Yrs	12.1	44.8	56.4	26.4	53.1	29.8	38.9
7 + Yrs	83.2	42.5	30.7	65.0	32.2	63.6	42.8
Total	100	100	100	100	100	100	100
N =	(195)	(469)	(464)	(404)	(412)	(396)	(573)
Female education							
None	2.2	15.7	20.1	5.7	20.2	9.7	22.1
1–6 Yrs	12.5	45.0	51.5	29.7	47.8	30.6	34.1
7 + Yrs	85.3	39.3	28.4	64.6	32.0	59.7	43.8
Total	100	100	100	100	100	100	100
N =	(195)	(469)	(464)	(404)	(412)	(396)	(573)

occupation, while GPS alone and LS & GPS are over twice as important.

The major portion of participation within these three programs is in agricultural occupations, which account for over 90 percent of non-household occupations (See Table 2.3). The agricultural employment generated by these programs is in stark contrast to the type of employment which characterizes the RE and RE & GPS programs. In the former, employment in 'Public Sector' occupations accounts for two-thirds of non-household employment, and in the latter about two-fifths.

Female Income. All the development programs, with the exception of GPS, exhibit a significant positive relationship with female income. The programs with the highest predictive value are GPS & RE, RE & LS, and RE alone. Each of these programs is a more important predictor of income than female educational attainment but a less important predictor than female non-household occupation. Once again, this would seem to suggest that RE plays an important role in the presence of another development program to increase the level of income.

Impacts of Development Programs on Fertility

The correlation coefficient between a development program and the average number of children born during the five years prior to interview measures the total effect of this program on recent fertility. This effect transmitted through change in socioeconomic characteristics of males and females is estimated by using path models. Three paths through which development programs have been hypothesized to affect fertility are: (1) through occupation and family planning, (2) through occupation, income and family planning, and (3) through income and family planning. These paths are presented in Figures 2.3 to 2.6. The path from family planning to fertility measures the effect of the use of contraception on fertility after controlling for the effect of duration of marriage. All the other paths measure the effect of antecedent variables after controlling for the effects of duration of marriage and education of males and females. The discussion which follows focusses on the significance and direction of relationship indicated by these paths.

Males. Figure 2.3 presents the paths for the individual development programs for males. The models for GPS and LS are similar in two respects. First, the path coefficients from occupation to family planning and occupation to income are not significant, and second, the paths indicating development effects through income and family planning on fertility are significant. However, the effect on fertility of GPS and LS through this latter path is positive because of the unexpected inverse relationship between income and family planning.

The path coefficient indicating the effect of occupation on family planning for the RE program is also not significant. In contrast to the GPS and LS programs the path coefficient measuring the effect of occupation on income is significant although it shows a positive relationship. The effects of RE on fertility through occupation, income and family planning and through income and family planning are also positive.

The path coefficients for the mixes of development programs are presented in Figure 2.4. The model for the GPS & RE program, as with the models for the individual programs, indicates that the effect of occupation on family planning is not significant. However, the remaining path coefficients are significant. GPS & RE decrease fertility through occupation, income and family planning, and through income and family planning alone.

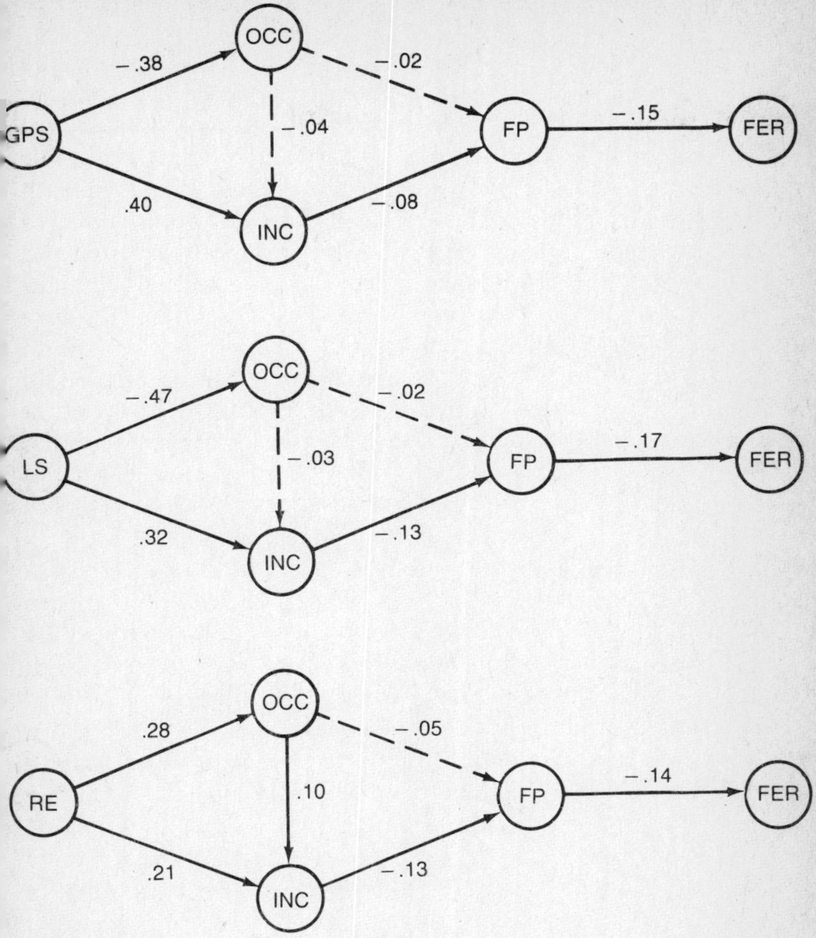

Key:

FER = fertility (births in the last five years)
FP = family planning
GPS = guaranteed price scheme
INC = income
LS = land settlement
OCC = occupation
RE = rural electrification

Note: A broken line indicates that the effect is not significant. A solid line indicates that the effect is significant at the .001 level.

Figure 2.3 Paths of relationship between *individual* development programs, *male* socioeconomic status, family planning and recent fertility

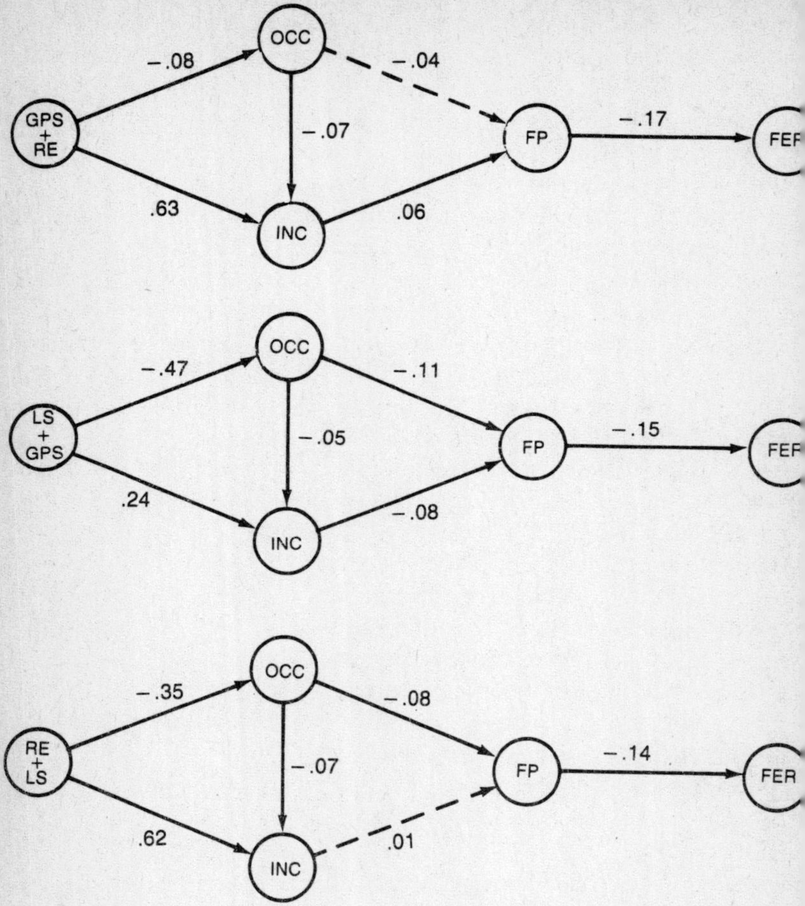

Key:

FER = fertility (births in the last five years)
FP = family planning
GPS = guaranteed price scheme
INC = income
LS = land settlement
OCC = occupation
RE = rural electrification

Note: A broken line indicates that the effect is not significant. A solid line indicates that the effect is significant at the .001 level.

Figure 2.4 Paths of relationship between *combination* of development programs, *male* socioeconomic status, family planning and recent fertility

The path coefficients indicating the effects of LS & GPS on fertility are all significant. However, only the path through occupation and family planning exerts a negative effect on fertility. This path also exerts a negative effect on fertility in the model for the RE & LS program. The remaining paths in the program which operate through income and family planning do not affect fertility because the path between these two variables is not significant.

In all three models for the mixes of development programs, participation in non-agricultural occupations shows a significant inverse relation with income. The individual programs with the exception of RE also show an inverse relationship but it is not significant. Although this relationship may be unexpected in some countries, it is consistent with findings for Sri Lanka as a whole. That is, in the rural sector the wages for 'Workers in Agriculture' are higher than the wages for 'Workers in Industry and Commerce', even taking into account seasonal variation (CBC, 1979).

The decomposition of the relationship between development programs and fertility is presented in Table 2.4. In comparison to the recent fertility of couples living in areas without any development program, couples benefiting from each of the three development programs exhibit a higher fertility. However, couples benefiting from any two programs exhibit a lower fertility than those living in areas without any development programs—GPS & RE exhibiting the largest total effect followed by LS & GPS and RE & LS, respectively. The major portion of these effects operates through occupation and family planning for the LS & GPS and RE & LS programs, and through income and family planning for the GPS & RE program.

Females. Figure 2.5 presents the path coefficients indicating the effects of the individual development programs on fertility through occupation and income of females. The models for GPS and LS indicate that the effect of female participation in non-household occupations on family planning is not significant. However, in both models the effect on fertility transmitted through occupation, income and family planning is significant and negative. In the LS model the effect on fertility transmitted through income and family planning is also significant and negative.

The RE model indicates that the effect of rural electrification on the participation of females in non-household occupations is not significant. Its effect on fertility transmitted through income and family planning is significant but positive.

Table 2.4 Decomposition (for males) of the indirect effect of development programs on fertility

Development Programs	Effect upon fertility			Total
	Via occupation and family planning	Via occupation, income and planning	Via income and family planning	
GPS	n.s.	n.s.	+ 0.005	+ 0.0050
LS	n.s.	n.s.	+ 0.007	+ 0.0070
RE	n.s.	+ 0.0005	+ 0.004	+ 0.0045
GPS & RE	n.s.	- 0.0001	- 0.006	- 0.0061
LS & GPS	- 0.008	+ 0.0003	+ 0.003	- 0.0047
RE & LS	- 0.004	n.s.	n.s.	- 0.0040

The path coefficients indicating the effects of the mixes of development programs are presented in Figure 2.6. The model for GPS & RE indicates all path coefficients are significant. Each of the paths through occupation and family planning, occupation, income and family planning, and income and family planning alone indicate a negative effect of these program outputs upon fertility.

In the LS & GPS program the effect of occupation on family planning is not significant. However, the effects of these programs on fertility transmitted through the two remaining paths are significant and negative.

The model for RE & LS indicates that the effect of income on family planning is not significant. However, the effect of these programs on fertility transmitted through occupation and family planning is significant.

Table 2.5 presents the results of the decomposition of the indirect effect of development programs on fertility through socioeconomic characteristics of females. GPS and LS & GPS exert the largest total negative effect on fertility followed by RE & LS and LS, respectively. The major portion of the total effects for the GPS, LS & GPS and LS programs operates through occupation, income and family planning. In the RE & LS programs the major effect operates through occupation and family planning.

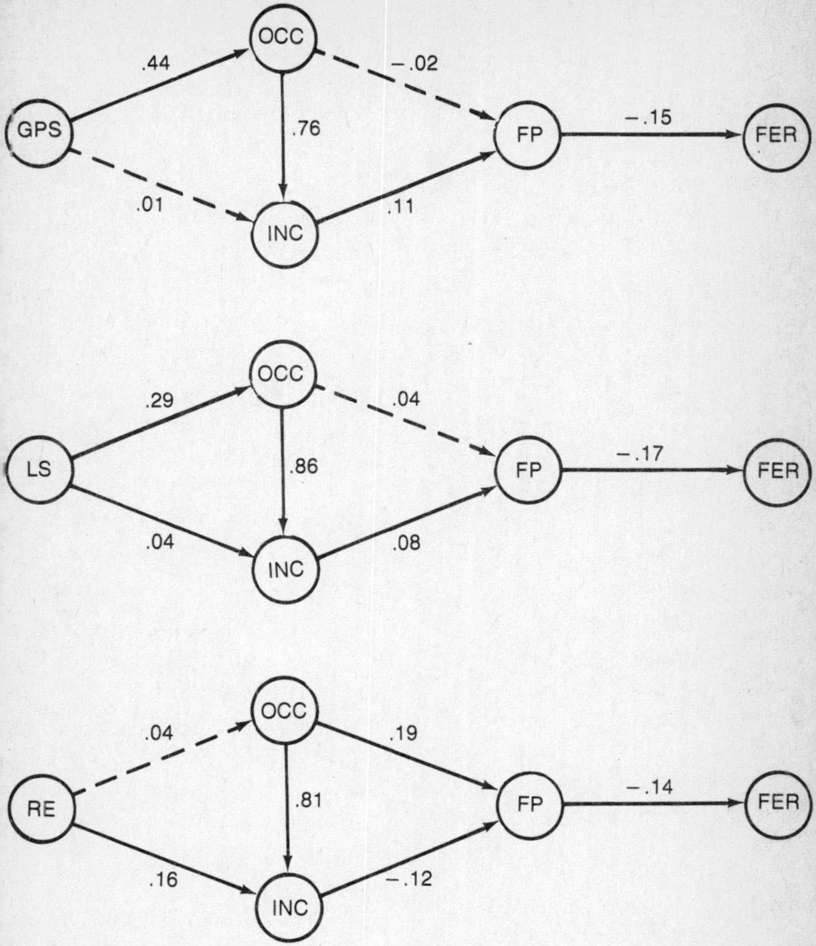

Key:

FER = fertility (births in the last five years)
FP = family planning
GPS = guaranteed price scheme
INC = income
LS = land settlement
OCC = occupation
RE = rural electrification

Note: A broken line indicates that the effect is not significant. A solid line indicates that the effect is significant at the .001 level.

Figure 2.5 Paths of relationship between *individual* development programs, *female* socioeconomic status, family planning and recent fertility

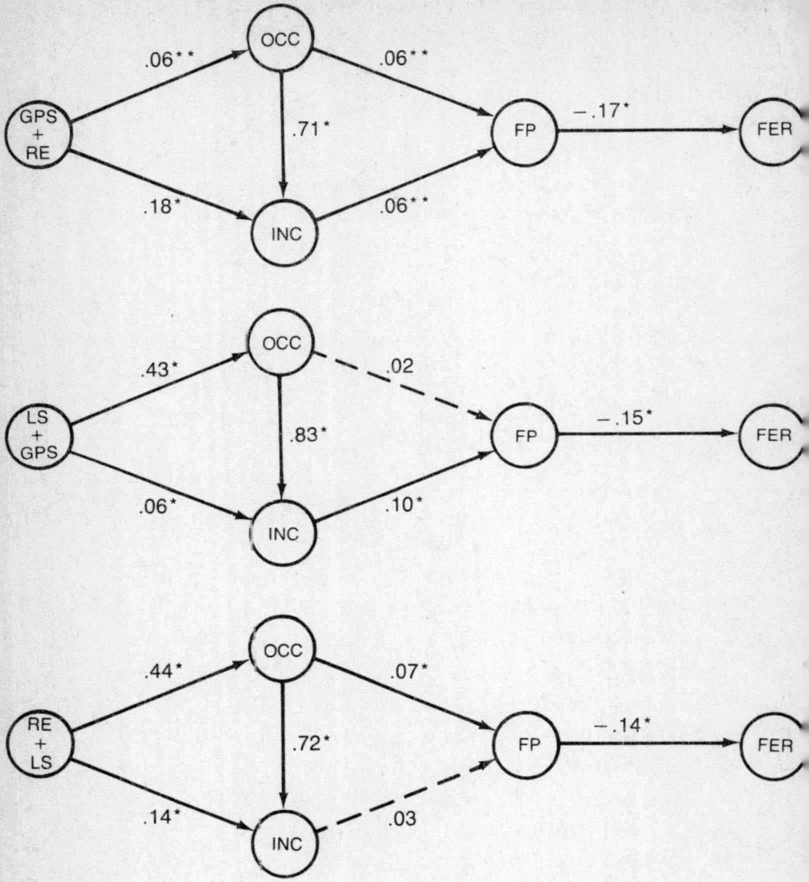

Key:

FER = fertility (births in the last five years)
FP = family planning
GPS = guaranteed price scheme
INC = income
LS = land settlement
OCC = occupation
RE = rural electrification

Note: A broken line indicates that the effect is not significant.

*Significant at the .001 level.
**Significant at the .01 level.

Figure 2.6 Paths of relationship between *combination* of development programs, *female* socioeconomic status, family planning and recent fertility

Table 2.5 Decomposition (for females) of the indirect effect of development programs on fertility

Development programs	Effect upon fertility			Total
	Via occupation and family planning	Via occupation, income and familyplanning	Via income and family planning	
GPS	n.s.	- 0.006	n.s.	- 0.0060
LS	n.s.	- 0.003	- 0.0005	- 0.0035
RE	n.s.	n.s.	0.003	+ 0.0030
GPS & RE	- 0.001	- 0.0004	- 0.0018	- 0.0032
LS & GPS	n.s.	- 0.005	- 0.0009	- 0.0059
RE & LS	0.004	n.s.	n.s.	- 0.0040

The results among four programs—GPS, LS & GPS, LS and GPS & RE—indicate that female income is directly related to practice of family planning. In an attempt to further refine the effects of female income, additional regressions for family planning were performed for these four programs, which included male income among the independent variables. The results, shown in Table 2.6, indicate that female income remains a significant and positive predictor of family planning net of the effects of female occupation, her education, duration of marriage and male income. The implications for this finding are discussed in the following section.

Conclusions

The analysis has supported the first portion of the general working hypothesis that development programs and their different combinations will exert an effect on the socioeconomic structure of a population. The second portion of the hypothesis which states that the socioeconomic structure will affect fertility through family planning is supported for all programs, either through the effect of occupation or income or both variables. Table 2.7 summarizes the effects for both parts of the hypothesis by a simple rank ordering of program impacts on male and female socioeconomic status and fertility. Several conclusions are drawn from this summary and the more specific results of the analysis discussed in the previous section.

Table 2.6 Standardized regression coefficients (betas) for family planning practice regressed on selected socioeconomic factors and marital duration by selected development programs, Sri Lanka, 1982

Independent Variables	Development Program GPS	LS	GPS&RE	LS&GPS
	Familyplanning practice			
Female non-household occupation	0.02	0.04	0.05	0.05
Female income	0.11*	0.08*	0.06**	0.10*
Male income	- 0.14*	- 0.15*	0.06**	- 0.10*
Female education	- 0.12*	- 0.07*	- 0.06*	- 0.07*
Marital duration	0.01	0.09*	0.12**	0.06*
R^2 =	0.03	0.04	0.04	0.04
N =	(1,041)	(1,037)	(975)	(985)

*Significant at 0.001
**Significant at 0.01

1. The effects of the programs and their mixes are gender specific. First, the magnitude of the program effects on income are not the same for males and females. All programs and their mixes make a greater contribution to increasing male income than they do to increasing female income net of their education and occupation. And second, the ranking of the effects of programs on income and fertility are not necessarily the same for males and females (see Table 2.7). Although the GPS & RE and the RE & LS programs exert the greatest effect upon male income and GPS & RE the greatest effect on female income, the RE program ranks second in its effect upon female income (tied with RE & LS) and sixth in its effect upon male income. In addition, the GPS program which ranks third in

its effect upon male income ranks sixth in its effect upon female income.

Table 2.7 Rank order of development program's effect upon socioeconomic factors and fertility by sex*

Rank	Male			Female		
	Non-Agricultural Occupation**	Income**	Fertility†	Non-Household Occupation**	Income**	Fertility‡
1.	(-)LS & GPS	GPS & RE	(-)GPS & RE	RE & LS	GPS & RE	(-)GPS
2.	(-)LS	RE & LS	(-)LS & GPS	GPS	RE	(-)LS & GPS
3.	(-)GPS	GPS	(-)RE & LS	LS & GPS	RE & LS	(-)RE & LS
4.	(-)RE & LS	LS	RE	LS	LS & GPS	LS
5.	RE	LS & GPS	GPS	GPS & RE	LS	GPS & RE
6.	(-)GPS & RE	RE	LS	RE §	GPS	RE

*(-) in the Table indicates negative relationship

** Rankings on the basis of absolute values rather than sign of development program beta coefficients from Table 2

† Rankings of the total effects of development programs on fertility from Table 4.

‡ Rankings of the total effects of development programs on fertility from Table 5

§ Not significant

As summarized in Table 2.7, the differences in program impacts on fertility transmitted through characteristics of males and females are even more striking. Only the three mixes of development programs show a negative effect on fertility through socioeconomic characteristics of males and family planning. However, all programs with the exception of RE exert a negative effect on fertility through socioeconomic characteristics of females. Hence, any attempt to disentangle the fertility effects of development programs must necessarily take into account their differential effects on males and females. This would be particularly important in interpreting or explaining analyses conducted at the household level where these differences are lost when constructing household indicators of socioeconomic status. In addition, the gender specific nature of program impacts should also be taken into account in any attempt to anticipate future changes in fertility.

2. Participation of females in occupations outside the household does not necessarily increase their practice of family planning methods. The models for the RE program and the two mixes of programs which include RE, i.e. RE & GPS and RE & LS, do show a positive effect of non-household occupations on the use of contraception. However, for the three remaining programs the relationship between occupation and contraceptive use is not significant. This would suggest that it is not simply employment outside the household that will increase family planning practice but the type of employment itself. This assertion gains partial support from an inspection of the distribution of the type of occupations between the RE programs and the other three programs (see Table 2.3) The former programs are characterized by participation of females in 'Public Sector' occupations, which account for two-thirds of the non-household occupations for RE; 40 percent for GPS & RE, and 10 percent for RE & LS. In the three remaining programs this proportion does not exceed 2 percent. Further, the practice of family planning among the 'Public Sector' occupations reaches almost 50 percent and is higher than in any of the remaining non-household occupations where practice is about 40 percent.

3. In contrast to male income which exerted an inverse effect on the practice of family planning methods in four of the six models, female income showed a positive effect on family planning in four of six models. The most important determinant of female income was her occupation, and the path that indicated the highest negative effect of development on fertility in three of the models was the path of the development program through female occupation, income and family planning. This would suggest that if the level of income of females were raised within the existing occupational structure, then levels of family planning would increase and contribute to lower fertility.

An internal constraint currently affecting the level of female income in the agricultural sector in Sri Lanka is the inequality of their wage rates with those of males within the same occupation. Results shown in Table 2.8 vividly illustrate this point with a comparison of average annual wage rates between sexes within the same agricultural occupations. Females earn from 19 to 39 percent less than males in paddy farming occupations; 29 to 36 percent less in coconut cultivation; 14 to 29 percent less in rubber cultivation; and 23 to 38 percent less in tea cultivation. Given these substantial differences, a policy directed at eliminating wage inequality should make a contribution to increasing the use of family planning methods and lowering fertility.

Table 2.8 Gender differences in average annual daily wage rates in rupees for occupations which include both sexes in paddy farming, coconut cultivation, rubber cultivation and tea cultivation in Sri Lanka, 1979

Agricultural sector and occupation	Male wage rate	Female wage rate	% difference
Paddy farming			
Ploughing	16	12	-25
Transplanting	15	11	-27
Weeding	14	11	-21
Harvesting	16	13	-19
Winnowing	18	11	-39
Coconut cultivation			
Planting	14	10	-29
Manuring	14	9	-36
Collecting nuts	13	9	-31
Rubber cultivation			
Planting	14	10	-29
Tapping	14	12	-14
Tea cultivation			
Preparation of land	13	8	-38
Planting	13	10	-23
Pruning	13	10	-23
Plucking	13	10	-23

Source: Statistics Department, Central Bank of Ceylon, 1979. *Price and Wage Statistics: Recent Trends in Retail, Producer and Input Prices and Wages*, December.

4. The indirect impact of development programs on fertility has been demonstrated for selected programs. Although these effects are significant, their magnitude is small. Since the path models have shown that development programs are generally strong predictors of socioeconomic status of both males and females, the problem with predicting fertility occurs with the portion of the model between socioeconomic status, family planning and fertility. Certainly a major part of this problem is the lack of proximate

determinants in addition to family planning included in the models for socioeconomic status to work through in its effect on fertility. This is highlighted by the amount of variation in fertility accounted for by the use of contraception and marital duration. On average, these two variables account for a quarter of the variations in recent fertility, leaving a substantial portion undetermined. The values of R^2 for each development program are: LS = 0.24; GPS = 0.26; RE = 0.25; LS & GPS = 0.24; RE & LS = 0.27; and GPS & RE = 0.26. Additional proximate determinants that may account for this variation would be the incidence and length of breastfeeding, induced abortion, and age at marriage. If occupation and income were positively related to these variables then additional negative effects on fertility would result. However, there are no data available on these relationships. Induced abortion is still illegal in Sri Lanka although a recent estimate by the Minister of Health places the rate at around five hundred per month. The WFS of 1975 found that the incidence and mean length of breastfeeding in the last closed interval varied inversely with women's educational attainment (Department of Census and Statistics, 1978). In the present study women's education varies directly with female income but inversely with female occupation. Hence, the effects on fertility of income as it operates through breastfeeding may be expected to be positive while the effects through occupation may be negative.

Age at marriage has been found to vary directly with women's educational attainment (Hodge and Ogawa, 1981); therefore, the effects on fertility of women's income and occupation as they operate through age at marriage would be negative and positive, respectively. However, these effects in the present study are expected to be minimal since we are not dealing with cumulative fertility but with fertility within a short period of five years.

Another factor affecting the results between the socioeconomic status, family planning and fertility portion of the models is the inverse relationship in several programs between male income and family planning. This finding and the inverse relationship between (female and male) education and family planning results in a positive effect on fertility of these variables.

The results for female education may be partially explained by the differential use between education groups of traditional family planning methods. The analysis of WFS data for Sri Lanka found that the 'use of traditional method only' increases with female education; and a decline in 'contraceptive method use score' between women with '10–11 years' of education and 'higher' education married for five years or more (Immerwahr, 1981). One explanation for this finding is that the higher educated females are more aware of the side effects of contraceptives, particularly the pill, and hence resort to traditional family planning methods.

Of particular note here, however, is that in four of the six models the use of contraception increased with female income net of the effect of her education and male income. This would appear to illustrate once again the importance of this factor relative to male income in increasing the practice of family planning methods and in decreasing fertility, but further research is necessary to analyze the dynamics of this relationship and its implications. For example, how is gender specific income allocated for expenditure within the household? How does gender specific income relate to decisionmaking among couples on matters of family size and contraceptive practice? More specifically, are females able to control the allocation and expenditure of their income, and through this control affect decisions regarding the sizes of their families?

References

Central Bank of Ceylon, Statistics Department, 1979. *Price and Wage Statistics; Recent Trends in Retail, Producer and Input Prices and Wages*, Vol. 1, No. 2, Colombo, Sri Lanka.

Central Bank of Ceylon, 1981. *Review of the Economy*. Central Bank, Colombo, Sri Lanka.

Department of Census and Statistics, 1974. *The Population of Sri Lanka*. Colombo, Sri Lanka.

Department of Census and Statistics, 1978. *World Fertility Survey—Sri Lanka: First Report*. Colombo, Sri Lanka.

Department of Census and Statistics, 1981. *Annual Paddy Statistics*. Government of Sri Lanka, Colombo, Sri Lanka.

Fernando, D., 1974. 'A Note on Differential Fertility in Sri Lanka.' *Demography*, **11**.

Goldberger, A. S., 1970. 'Boudon's Method of Linear Causal Analysis.' *American Sociological Review*,**35**.

GSL, 1970. *Report of the Commissioner of Agrarian Services*. Government of Sri Lanka, Colombo, Sri Lanka.

GSL, 1979. *Administrative Report of the Land Commissioner*. Colombo, Sri Lanka.

GSL, 1980. *Report of the Central Electricity Board: List of Rural Electrification Programs, 1961–1979*. Colombo, Sri Lanka.

Government of Sri Lanka, 1981. *Annual Report of the Paddy Marketing Board*. Colombo, Sri Lanka.

GSL, 1982. *Administrative Reports of the Director of Irrigation*, 1975–1981. Colombo, Sri Lanka.

Hanna, B. and Madarajah, T., 1976. 'Some Aspects of Fertility Differentials in Sri Lanka,' in *Population Problems of Sri Lanka*. Demographic Training and Research Unit, University of Sri Lanka, Colombo.

Hodge, R. & Ogawa, N., 1981. 'Fertility and Marriage in Sri Lanka: Some Insights from Path Analysis,' NUPRI Research Paper Series, No. 6.

Immerwahr, G., 1981. 'Contraceptive Use in Sri Lanka.' *WFS Scientific Reports*, No. 18.

Kumaraswamy, S., 1956. *Fertility Trends in Ceylon*. Monograph No. 8, Department of Census and Statistics, Colombo, Sri Lanka.

Langford, C. M., 1981. 'Fertility Change in Sri Lanka Since the War: An Analysis of Different Districts.' *Population Studies*, **14**.

Langford, C. M., 1982. 'The Fertility of Tamil Estate Workers in Sri Lanka.' *Scientific Reports*, WFS, London.

Little, R. & Perera, Soma, 1981. 'Illustrative Analysis: Socio-Economic Differentials in Cumulative Fertility in Sri Lanka—A Marriage Cohort Approach.' *Scientific Reports*, No. 12, WFS, London.

Raja, Indra R., 1954. *Fertility Trends in Ceylon*. Monograph No. 3, Department of Census and Statistics, Colombo, Sri Lanka.

Sarkar, N. K., 1954. *The Demography of Sri Lanka*. Ceylon Government Press, Colombo, Sri Lanka.

3 Fertility Effects of Electrification in Northeast Thailand

*Suwanlee Piampiti**

Introduction

The Problem and Objectives

The benefit to a country's development resulting from rural electrification programs is well known. Electrification can play a critical role in irrigation by providing a cheaper source of energy than petrol for pumps to lift water from rivers, canals, lakes, tube wells and open wells (United Nations, 1963, pp. 34–5). It can contribute to employment in and development of small-scale village industries such as village workshops for the manufacture and repair of agricultural implements and the maintenance of vehicles, carpentry shops, sawmills, and storage and refrigeration warehouses for agricultural produce (United Nations, 1954, p. 35). In addition, electrification has been found to contribute to increased agricultural labor productivity because farm families can do housework, and cook and eat in the darkness of the early morning and evening, leaving more daylight time for agricultural activities (Office of Rural Electrification, 1977, p. 115).

Although rural electrification as a development program is pursued primarily for these non-demographic types of benefits, it may also contribute to a demographic benefit (Herrin, 1979), i.e. lower fertility, through its effect on the socioeconomic structure of a population. A recent study in Misamis Oriental, Philippines, found an association between rural electrification and large increases in new business and off-farm employment, change in occupational pattern, increase in cash and real income, and decline in fertility (Madigan, 1982, p. 21). Research on the impact of accessibility of family planning services on contraceptive use in

* National Institute of Development Administration

Thailand found a positive association between rural electrification and use of contraception (Napaporn *et al.*, 1984). Another study conducted in Thailand in only two villages suggested an inverse relationship between electrification and fertility (M. Pehanan, 1982).

The present investigation focusses on an analysis of the linkages between electrification and fertility. Specifically, the objective of this study is to analyze the relationship between rural electrification, socioeconomic structure, and the fertility of the population in the Northeast region of the country. This is done by comparing couples living in villages which have electricity and those living in villages without electricity.

Rural Electrification Program

The Provincial Electricity Authority (PEA), established in 1960, is responsible for supplying electrical power for residential, commercial and industrial consumption throughout the country, with the exception of the Bangkok metropolitan area. Because of increasing demand for electricity and the government's recognition of the critical role played by electrification in economic development, the PEA initiated a new approach to electrification in 1970 with the creation of the Accelerated Rural Electrification (ARE) Program. However, it was not until 1974 that the ARE Program became formally established under the newly created Office of Rural Electrification (ORE) set up with the approval of the PEA Board of Directors. The total plan for the programs consisted of five five-year consecutive short-range programs, each overlapping by two years, resulting in a total program period beginning in 1977 of fifteen years (National Energy Administration, 1977).

The first of the five programs was implemented in the Northeast where the proportion of households with electricity in 1976 was only 12 percent, the lowest proportion of the four regions of the country. Through the ARE program this proportion increased to almost 75 percent by the end of 1981, representing a substantial portion of the population in the 5,200 villages targeted for completion of electrification by 1983 (Provincial Electricity Authority, 1981).

Population and Family Planning in the Northeast

The Northeast is the largest of four geographic regions in Thailand and accounts for over one-third of the country's population of approximately 50 million (Department of Local Government, 1981). Compared to the other regions it has the highest proportion of rural population, at over 90 percent (National Economic and Social Development Board, 1981); one of the highest rates of population growth at 2.5 percent in 1980 resulting from crude birth and death-rates of 32 and 7 respectively (Suchart & Tawatchai, 1980); and the highest rate of outmigration (National Statistical Office, 1981). The region is also the poorest in the country, with an annual per capita income of about $175 in 1978 (National Economic and Social Development Board, 1981) and the highest level of rural poverty estimated at 36 percent of the rural population in 1975–6 (Boonpratuang, 1980).

Because of the high level of poverty in the Northeast, the Thai government has targeted areas of the region for increased development and family planning inputs. These inputs have included larger numbers of rural development project offices which provide agricultural development assistance, i.e. subsidized seeds, fertilizers and livestock; and increased numbers of village health volunteers (VHVs) and village health communicators (VHCs) who are responsible for the delivery of family planning services and the provision of health care information (Government of Thailand, 1981).

In addition to these government inputs, the Population and Community Development Association (PDA) of Thailand, a private sector organization, has conducted programs which provide a package of developmental inputs aimed at increasing skills and productive capacity in agriculture and livestock; and which raise the acceptance level of family planning practice through the provision of these inputs. Included among the inputs are animal raising (e.g. pigs and commercial and village chickens); and the provision of crop marketing funds, seeds and fertilizers, rainwater tanks, wells, latrines, biogas digesters and crop storage of facilities (Stoeckel *et al.*, 1984).

According to the Contraceptive Prevalence Survey of 1981, the proportions of married women aged 15–44 currently practising family planning in the Northeast was about 55 percent. This rate was lower than either the North or Central region but higher than the rate for the Southern region (Peerasit and Apichat, 1982).

Conceptual Framework

The conceptual framework utilized in this study is presented in Figure 3.1. The working hypothesis of this framework is that fertility is indirectly affected by development, i.e. availability and utilization of electrification and other development programs alters the socioeconomic structure of household members which affects norms of family size, the intermediate variables, and ultimately fertility. Specifically, the availability of electricity contributes to the establishment of new agri-centered industries and generates opportunities for employment in both farm and non-farm type occupations which may enable females to participate in production. The new types of employment, particularly for females, should create alternative occupational roles for women and may lead ultimately to an improvement in their social status. This is expected to affect women's allocation of time within households, making less time available for raising children. This factor, in addition to the less labor-intensive methods of production made possible by electrification, for example pump extraction of water as opposed to manually obtaining and hauling water by children, reduces the utility of children for their labour. The expected increase in household income coupled with these factors would result in decreased demand for children, lower family size norms, higher practice of family planning and lower fertility.

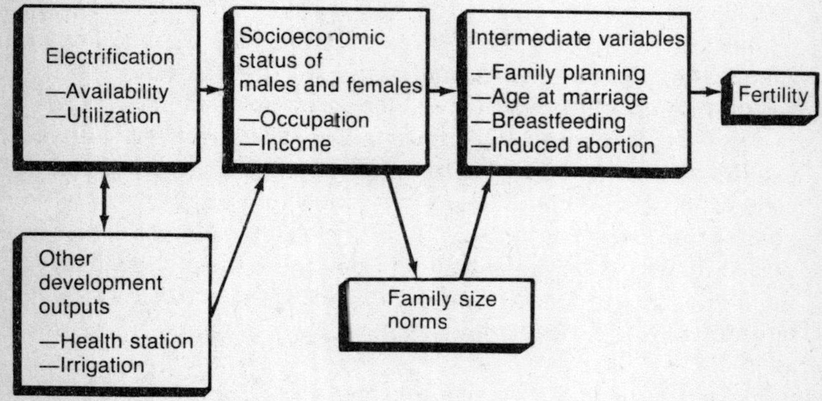

Figure 3.1 Conceptual framework for analyzing fertility impacts of electrification

Methodology

Two sources of data are utilized for the study, the first from conventional interviews with married women 15–44 years of age included in the sample, and the second from intensive interviews with a sub-sample of women included in the sample population. Data from the first source include information on socioeconomic factors, norms of family size, family planning and fertility. The second source of data focusses on information on the household time allocation of women and children, including time spent in household and non-household work activities, the types of activities, and their output.

Sample Design

The sample design consisted of four stages:

1. A sample of six provinces is drawn randomly from the total of sixteen provinces of the Northeast region.
2. A random sample of three districts is drawn from each of the two largest provinces (Khon Kaen and Udorn Thani), while two districts are selected randomly from the remaining four provinces, resulting in a total of fourteen districts.
3. All the villages of the fourteen districts are stratified into two groups, those with electricity and those without. From each of the two groups, a hundred villages are selected by simple random sampling.
4. A simple random sample of twenty-five households is drawn from a listing of households for each village, resulting in a total of five thousand households. All eligible married couples (women in reproductive ages) are interviewed. In addition, every fifth household is selected for an 'intensive' interview of the wife regarding time allocation for household work and production of herself and her children.

The sample design is summarized in Table 3.1.

Table 3.1 Summary cf sample design

Stratum	No. of villages	No. of households selected by SRS from each village	Total households	20% sample of total households for intensive interview
Electrified	100	25	2,500	500
Unelectrified	100	25	2,500	500
Total	200	50	5,000	1,000

Data Collection

The fieldwork for data collection (including the intensive interviews) was conducted during the period May–July 1981, by two teams of ten interviewers and two supervisors. Editing of interview schedules was conducted concurrently in the field as interviews took place.

Operational Definition of Variables

The operational definitions of the variables are as follows:

1. Development program outputs
   a) number of years electricity has been available in a village;
   b) household utilization of electricity;
   c) presence of a health station in a village;
   d) presence of an irrigation system in a village.
2. Socioeconomic status
   a) males—employment in non-agricultural occupations, and number of years of school completed;
   b) females—employment in non-agricultural occupations, and number of years of school completed;
   c) household income—average combined monthly income of household members.

3. Norms of family size
   a) the total number of children desired.
4. Intermediate variables
   a) the current practice of family planning;
   b) number of months of breastfeeding of the last child born.
5. Fertility
   a) the number of live births five years prior to the survey.

Results and Discussion

Characteristics of Sample Villages and Households

As seen in Table 3.2, electrified villages are generally more developed than unelectrified villages. A higher proportion of electrified villages have piped water, bus transportation, primary schools and women's organizations than unelectrified villages. However, more striking differences are apparent between villages when they are compared on the basis of concrete roads, health facilities and family planning centers. The proportions of electrified villages with roads and family planning centers are two times greater than the proportions of unelectrified villages, while the proportions with health stations are three times greater.

Table 3.3 presents a summary of the variables utilized in the analysis for households in electrified and unelectrified villages. In electrified villages twice the proportion of households have males and females employed in non-agricultural occupations than in unelectrified villages; and mean annual household income is higher in electrified than in unelectrified villages. Desired family size and breastfeeding is only slightly lower in households in electrified villages; and the incidence of family planning is higher and the level of fertility lower in households in electrified than in unelectrified villages.

The remaining portion of this section is divided into two parts. The first part presents the results of multiple regression analyses of the effects of electrification and other development indicators on male and female occupational status, and household income. The second part presents the results of multiple regression analyses which illustrate the relationships and links between development programs, socioeconomic status, intermediate variables and fertility. The rationale for presenting the analysis in this order is that

Table 3.2 Proportions of electrified and unelectrified sample villages with selected characteristics

Characteristics	Type of village Electrified %	 Unelectrified %
Piped water	36.7	26.4
Concrete road	65.0	29.2
Mini bus transportation	63.3	77.7
Bus transportation	51.7	45.8
Health station	40.0	13.9
Family planning center	21.7	11.1
Primary school	68.0	65.7
Cooperative society	48.3	56.9
Women's organization	31.7	19.4
N =	60	72

Table 3.3 Socio-economic and demographic characteristics of households in electrified and unelectrified villages

Characteristics	Electrified villages	Unelectrified villages
Proportion of males employed in non-agricultural occupations	26.20	10.90
Proportion of females employed in non-agricultural occupations	23.60	11.10
Mean annual household income (in dollars)	978.00	842.00
Mean desired family size	3.50	3.70
Mean number of months of breastfeeding of last child	20.20	20.90
Proportions ever using family planning	68.80	61.90
Mean number of births in past five years	0.65	0.72
N =	2,490	2,496

the impact of rural electrification and other development programs on fertility is necessarily indirect, operating through changes in socioeconomic status which affect the demand for children and intermediate variables. Without a demonstration of the former effects it would make little sense to continue with an analysis of the latter effects. In this analysis selected village characteristics are utilized as well as household and couple characteristics. The village characteristics are assigned to the sample of couples selected from the village. For example, those couples living in villages with electricity were assigned scores according to the number of years electricity had been available in the village and those living in villages without electricity received a score of zero. Similarly, scores on household characteristics such as utilization or non-utilization of electricity were assigned to couples of the household.

Impacts of Electrification on Socio-economic Status

Male and Female Occupation. Table 3.4 indicates that both period of availability of electricity in the village, and household utilization of electricity have a significant positive effect on male participation in non-agricultural occupations net of the effect of the irrigation and health inputs, and wife's educational attainment. Household utilization of electricity is twice as important a predictor of male occupation as period of availability of electricity at the village level.

The major impacts of electrification on the male occupational structure occur among 'Laborer,' 'Trading,' and 'Government' occupations (see Table 3.5). The proportions employed in these occupations are about three times higher among households with electricity than households without electricity. Furthermore, the proportion of males employed in these occupations and as 'Industrial Laborers' increases substantially with period of availability of electricity in villages. In villages with no electrification the proportions in these occupations never exceed 5 percent. However, by the time villages have been electrified for 10 to 19 years the proportions employed in 'Government' reach about 19 percent; and for villages electrified for twenty years or more the proportions employed in 'Trading' reach 20 percent, while the proportions employed as 'Laborers' and 'Industrial Laborers' reach about 15 and 10 percent, respectively.

Table 3.4 Summary of multiple regression analyses of the effect of development indicators upon socioeconomic factors

Independent variables	Male occupation	Female occupation	Household income
	Beta coefficients		
Village electrification (years)	0.08*	0.08*	0.01
Household use of electricity	0.17*	0.15*	0.07*
Health station	-0.05*	0.02	0.00
Irrigation	0.02	0.02	0.00
Wife's education	0.24*	0.26*	0.19*
Husband's occupation			0.21*
Wife's occupation			0.11*
R^2 =	0.11	0.11	0.15
N = (4,986)			

*Significant at < 0.05

Table 3.5 Percentage distribution of male occupations by electrification of households, and period of availability of electricity (in years) in villages

Husband's occupation	Period of availability of electricity in the village						
	Households		Years				
	Electrified Yes	No	0	1–4	5–9	10–19	20+
Agriculture	70.2	89.2	87.9	80.5	75.1	51.8	54.5
Fishery	0.6	0.6	0.6	0.8	-	0.3	-
Agriculture laborer	0.4	1.0	1.1	0.5	0.4	-	0.8
Industrial laborer	0.8	0.1	0.1	0.4	0.2	-	9.7
Laborer	12.0	3.9	4.5	8.5	10.1	15.5	14.9
Trading	5.8	2.0	2.0	2.1	6.7	13.6	20.1
Government employee	9.4	3.0	3.6	5.8	7.1	18.8	-
Cottage industry	0.8	0.2	0.2	1.4	0.4	-	-
Total	100.0	100.0	100.0	100.0	100.0	100.0	100.0
N =	(2,032)	(2,862)	(2,496)	(1,398)	(536)	(330)	(134)

Period of availability of electricity in the village and household utilization of electricity also exert a significant positive effect on female employment in non-agricultural occupations, with the latter predictor being about twice as important as the former predictor (See Table 3.4). The portion of the non-agricultural occupational structure which receives the major impact of these factors is employment in 'Trading' and 'Government' occupations. The proportions in these occupations are higher in households with electricity than in households without electricity; and generally increase monotonically from villages with no electricity to villages with electricity for twenty years or more, reaching levels of about 20 and 10 percent, respectively (see Table 3.6).

Table 3.6 Percentage distribution of female occupations by electrification of households, and period of availability of electricity (in years) in villages.

Wife's occupation	Households		Period of availability of electricity in village Years				
	Electrified Yes	No	0	1–4	5–9	10–19	20+
Agriculture	74.4	88.3	88.1	82.4	78.4	55.2	53.3
Fishery	0.4	0.4	0.4	0.4	-	0.3	-
Agricultural laborer	0.4	0.6	0.8	0.5	0.2	0.3	1.5
Industrial laborer	0.3	0.2	0.1	0.4	-	-	-
Laborer	3.3	2.4	2.2	2.5	3.3	5.8	2.9
Trading	9.3	2.6	2.5	3.7	8.4	20.9	19.7
Government employee	2.4	0.5	0.6	1.2	1.9	3.9	9.5
Cottage industry	1.5	0.7	0.7	2.3	0.2	0.6	2.2
Housewife	8.0	4.3	4.6	6.6	7.6	13.0	10.9
Total	100.0	100.0	100.0	100.0	100.0	100.0	100.0
N =	(2,032)	(2,862)	(2,496)	(1,401)	(538)	(330)	(137)

Household Income. The beta coefficients shown in column (3) of Table 3.4 indicate that household income increases with wife's education, participation of both husbands and wives in non-agricultural occupations, and household utilization of electricity. Both period of availability of electricity at the village level and its utilization at the household level increase household income indirectly by increasing participation of males and females in non-agricultural occupations. (These indirect relationships are depicted by a diagram containing boxes and arrows in Table 3.4. This diagram is equivalent to a path diagram.) The magnitude of an indirect effect of, for example, village electrification on household income can be estimated by multiplying two beta coefficients 0.08 and 0.21 for the impact associated with male occupations; and 0.08 and 0.11 for the impact associated with female occupation. The total indirect effect of village electrification on household income is the sum of these two quantities. Household utilization of electricity, in addition to this indirect effect, also increases household income directly, a portion of which represents *new* income-generating activities made possible by the household utilization of electricity. These activities include sewing, craftwork, home industry and sales of these products which produced increases in average monthly female income (See Table 3.7). Hence, utilization of household electricity may have provided more time to engage in these activities, i.e. through lighting to work in evenings, as well as facilitated some of the activities, for example, the use of electric sewing machines.

Table 3.7 Proportion of households engaged in new income generating activities after electrification became available.

Type of activity	Percentage
Sewing	15.7
Craftwork	17.1
Home industry	14.8
Activities related to animal raising	4.6
Activities related to farming	3.8
Sales	24.9
Other	19.1
Total	100.0
(Number)	(345)
Average increase in monthly income from activities	67 Baht

Support for this assertion is suggested by the results of the sub-sample of data collected on the household time allocation of female activities. The hours spent in 'wage work' and 'trading' (activities which include the activities referred to above) by women in electrified households during both the 'peak' and 'slack' agricultural seasons is two times greater than the hours spent by women in households without electricity (See Table 3.8).

Table 3.8 Mean number of person hours per day spent in selected activities by females during 'peak' and 'slack' agricultural seasons in electrified and unelectrified households.

Activities	Electrified households	Unelectrified households
	Mean number of hours	
Peak season		
Wage work	201	46
Trading	242	142
Slack season		
Wage work	538	262
Trading	695	199
N =	(501)	(483)

Impacts of Electrification on Fertility

The relationship between electrification, socioeconomic status, intermediate variables, and fertility is illustrated in Table 3.9. There are three patterns of linkages through which village level availability of electricity and household utilization of electricity exhibit a significant antinatalistic effect on fertility. The first is through the positive effect of male non-agricultural occupation on family planning which is inversely related to fertility; and the second and third are through the negative effects of male and female non-agricultural occupations on desired family size which inversely affects the use of family planning methods (see diagram in Table 3.9). Surprisingly, the effects of household income on desired family size or the use of family planning methods are not significant. Although the effect of household income on the duration of breastfeeding is significant, its effect on the recent fertility is not. For this reason, various other indirect effects of electrification on fertility transmitted through household income and/or breastfeeding are not significant and as such not shown in the diagram in Table 3.9.

Table 3.9 Summary of multiple regression analyses of the effect of rural electrification on fertility as it operates through effects on socioeconomic status and intermediate variables.

Independent variables	Husband's occupation	Wife's occupation	Household income	Desired family size	Breast-feeding	Family planning	Fertility
	Beta coefficients						
Village electrification (Yrs)	0.08*	0.08*	0.01				
Household use of electricity	0.17*	0.15*	0.07*				
Health station	-0.05*	0.02	0.00				
Irrigation	0.02	0.02	0.00				
Wife's education	0.24*	0.26*	0.19*	-0.13*	-0.12*	0.04*	
Husband's occupation			0.21*	-0.08*	-0.09*	0.06*	
Wife's occupation			0.11*	-0.05*	0.01	0.00	
Household income				0.03	0.05*	0.00	
Desired family size						-0.03*	
Breastfeeding							0.03
Family planning							-0.10*
Duration of marriage				0.25*	0.01	-0.17*	-0.44*
R^2	0.11	0.11	0.15	0.10	0.03	0.03	0.18
(N = 4,986)							

*Significant at < 0.05

The finding that desired family size is affected by electrification via occupation is expected. However, as discussed under the conceptual framework, desired family size may also be affected by the reduction in utility of children for their labor through less labor-intensive methods of production made possible by electrification. Although we cannot test this hypothesis directly, the subsample of data on women's time allocation does include information on children's time and participation in work activities which provides some evidence suggesting support; that is, in electrified households children of both sexes were found to have consistently lower rates of participation (the rates were lowest for females) in both household and economic work activities than children in households with no electricity (see Table 3.10). Household work activities include cutting firewood, rice cooking, food preparation, gathering vegetables and fetching water; and economic work activities include threshing, transplanting, harvesting and cattle raising. Hence, this suggests that electrification may play a contributing role in reducing the utility of children for work in these activities.

Table 3.10 Proportions of children aged 11–15 years participating in household and economic work activities by sex in electrified and unelectrified households

Activities	Electrified		Unelectrified	
	Male	Female	Male	Female
Household work				
Cutting firewood	43	49	49	55
Rice cooking	44	75	46	76
Food preparation	19	50	26	61
Gathering vegetables	49	54	49	64
Fetching water	66	81	68	85
Economic work				
Threshing	4	1	5	4
Transplanting	14	18	17	22
Harvesting	9	12	12	18
Cattle raising	41	18	49	36
N =	(255)	(274)	(239)	(256)

The lack of relationship between household income and the use of family planning methods reflects homogeneity in the use of family planning methods across different income levels. This is supported by the data on income and contraceptive practice presented in Table 3.11. Excluding the lowest income group (<5,000 Baht) which has the lowest proportion of respondents (5 percent), the greatest difference between any two of the remaining seven income categories is no more than 3.4 percentage points. Therefore, it would appear that in this sample of villages in Northeast Thailand a relatively uniform level of family planning practice across income groups has been achieved.

Table 3.11 Percent of contraceptive practice by level of household income

Household income (In Baht per year)	%
<5,000	43.1
5,000–9,999	50.6
10,000–14,999	49.8
15,000–19,999	50.8
20,000–24,999	50.5
25,000–29,999	47.9
30,000–39,999	51.5
40,000 +	48.1
Total	50.1
N = 4,894	

Conclusions

The general working hypothesis of the study, that electrification alters the socioeconomic structure of household members which affects norms of family size, the intermediate variables and ultimately fertility, has been supported by the results of the analysis presented in this chapter. Two patterns of fertility effects of electrification were found. The first showed that village-level availability and household utilization of electricity exerted a positive effect on employment of males and females in non-agricultural occupations, which exerted a negative effect on desired family size. This latter factor was inversely related to family planning practice, and because practice was inversely related to fertility, the total effect on fertility by electrification is negative.

The second pattern of effects was through the impact of the two indicators of electrification on male occupation which was directly related to family planning. This also resulted in a negative effect on fertility.

The beta coefficients from the multivariate analysis which document these linkages in the relationship between rural electrification and fertility are significant and in the direction hypothesized. Further, the findings from the in-depth study of a sub-sample of women tend to corroborate and provide additional basis for the linkages identified by the multivariate analysis between electrification, occupation and norms of family size. The in-depth study found that electrification was associated with (1) changes in female occupation which resulted in greater participation of females in wage work and trading; and (2) changes in the participation of children in household and economic activities which reduced their utility as labor and may have contributed to lower desired family sizes. Clearly, the combination of these findings with the multivariate analyses suggests that changes in the occupational structure produced by electrification at both the village and household level for males and females can exert an antinatalistic impact on fertility through changes in norms of family size and the use of family planning methods. Consequently, continued development efforts in the area of rural electrification will be expected to contribute to a decline in fertility in Thailand.

References

Boonpratuang, Chet, 1980. 'Analyses of Fertility Differentials at the Regional Level. Research Paper (mimeo), Population and Manpower Planning Division, National Economic and Social Development Board.

Department of Local Government, 1981. Statistical Yearbook 1980. Ministry of Interior, Bangkok.

Government of Thailand, 1981. *The Fifth National Economic and Social Development Plan 1982–1986*. National Economic and Social Development Board, Office of the Prime Minister, Bangkok, Thailand.

Herrin, Alejandro N., 1979. 'Rural Electrification and Fertility Change in the Southern Philippines.' *Population and Development Review*, **5**, No. 1, pp. 61–86.

Madigan, F. C., 1982. 'Rural Electrification and Development.' Research Institute for Mindanao Culture, Xavier University, Cagayan de Oro City, Philippines.

Napaporn, Chayovan, Knodel, J., Nibhon, D., Aprichat, C. & Hermalin, A., 1984. 'The Impact of Accessibility on Contraceptive Use in Rural Thailand.' Final Report to The Population Council for Family Planning Operations Research Award.

National Economic and Social Development Board, 1981. *Thailand Social Indicators 1978–1980*. NESDB, Bangkok.

National Statistical Office, 1981. 'Survey of Migration in Bangkok 1977–1980.' Office of the Prime Minister, Bangkok.

Peerasit, K. and Apichat, C., 1982. *A New Decade of Fertility and Family Planning in Thailand: 1981 Contraceptive Prevalence Survey*, NIDA, Ministry of Public Health, and Westinghouse Health Systems, Bangkok, Thailand.

Pehanan, M., 1982. 'Impact of Village Electrification in Northern Thailand on Fertility,' in Suchart Prasithrathsint (ed.), *Fertility and Development Interactions in Thailand*. Steering and Review Committee, Microlevel Studies Program on Population and Development Interactions in Thailand.

Prasith-rathsint, Suchart and Arthornthurasook, Tawatchai, 1980. 'A Feasibility Study of Reducing Population Growth Rate to 1.5 Percent Per Annum by the End of the Fifth Five-Year Plan: Technical Demographic Analysis.' *Journal of Development Administration*, **20**, No. 3, p. 416.

Stoeckel, J., Fisher, A. A., Viravaidya, M. & NaPattalung, R., 1984. 'Increasing Family Planning Acceptance through Development Programs: An Experimental Study in Northeastern Thailand.' Regional Research Paper, South and East Asia, The Population Council, Bangkok, Thailand.

Thailand, National Energy Administration, 1977. 'Electric Power in Thailand.' Ministry of Science, Technology and Energy, Bangkok.

Thailand, Office of Rural Electrification, 1977. 'Rural Village Directory.' Provincial Electricity Authority, Bangkok.

Thailand, Provincial Electricity Authority, 1981. Annual Report.

United Nations, 1954. 'Rural Electrification.' New York.

United Nations, 1963. 'Rural Electrification in Asia and the Far East.' New York.

4 Fertility Effects of Agricultural Irrigation in Northeast Thailand

*Suchart Prasith-rathsint, Kanikar Sookasame, Laddawan Roodmanee and Manu Srikhagorn**

Introduction

The Problem and Objectives

Despite the considerable progress in economic growth and diversification of its economy during the past two decades, Thailand is still an agricultural country with the majority of its population earning their living from agricultural activities. Recognizing that agriculture remains a significant sector of the economy, the Thai government has made major investments in agricultural development. Among the agricultural inputs, irrigation has been singled out as one of the most important for development, particularly in the Northeastern region where the annual rainfall is the lowest and the proportion of rural population the highest among the four regions in the country.

The implementation of these agricultural irrigation systems could be expected to affect the demographic behavior of a population through affecting its socioeconomic structure. For example, the lack of an adequate water supply has contributed to the rural populations' encroachment on reserved forest areas, migration to urban or other rural areas for employment, and landlessness. In contrast, agricultural irrigation systems can provide temporary employment during the construction phase of the system, and greater farm employment opportunities after its completion. Employment, in turn, may affect family size decisions, the practice of contraception and ultimately fertility. Thus far, no attempt has been made to assess these relationships in Thailand. Therefore, the objective of this study is to estimate the effects of agricultural irrigation systems

* All with the National Institute of Development Administration

on socioeconomic factors, and fertility in the Northeast region of the country.

Agricultural Irrigation

Agricultural irrigation projects are implemented by the Royal Irrigation Department, and the Ministries of Interior, Agriculture, and Cooperatives. These projects are classified into three categories:

1. 'Large'—refers to a reservoir and irrigation system which costs a hundred million Baht of investment by the Government, each covering an area of several districts and provinces;
2. 'Medium'—refers to tank irrigation projects which cost tens of million Baht of investment and generally covers an area of a few villages; and
3. 'Small'—refers to a small dam and a farm pond which costs a million Baht or less, covering an area of a village.

As of 1979 in the Northeast, 3.2 percent of the region's 15,537 villages were under 'large' irrigation projects, and 2.5 and 1.5 percent under 'medium' and 'small' projects, respectively (Royal Irrigation Department, 1979).

Conceptual Framework

The conceptual framework utilized for this study is presented in Figure 4.1. The working hypothesis of this framework is that the availability and utilization of irrigation systems in combination with other development projects alters the social and economic structure of households, which affects norms of family size, the intermediate variables and consequently fertility. Specifically, irrigation contributes to a more effective land use pattern, higher cropping intensity and increases farm production, which results in higher household income. In addition, labor utilization within the household is altered and opportunities for female labor force participation in occupations outside the household are increased. The increased income and female labor force participation are then expected to decrease the demand for children, resulting in lower norms of family size, higher practice of family planning and lower fertility.

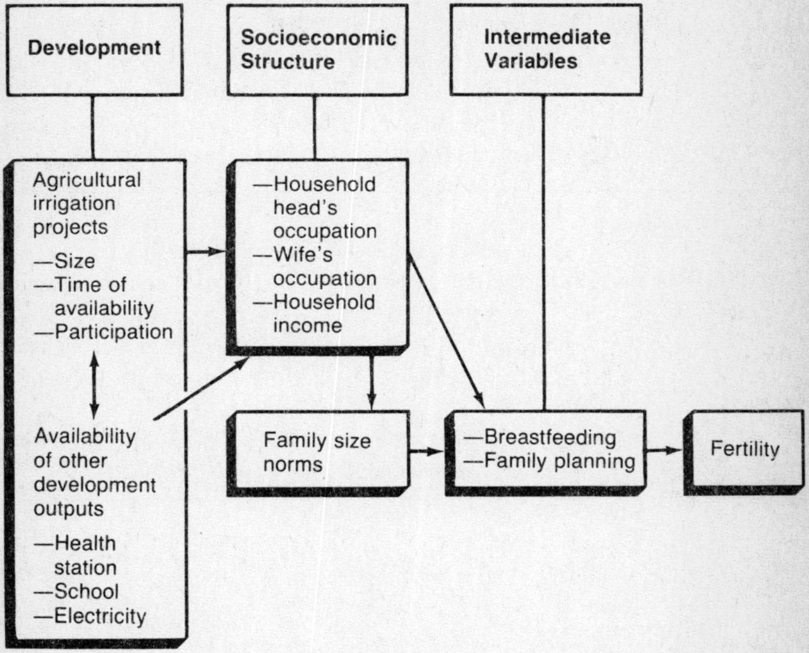

Figure 4.1 Conceptual framework for the interrelationship between agricultural irrigation projects and fertility

Methodology

Sample Design

All villages in the Northeastern region of Thailand were stratified into four groups on the basis of the size and existence of agricultural irrigation projects. These groups are: villages characterized by 'large,' 'medium' and 'small' projects, defined earlier, and those villages with 'no irrigation projects.'

From each of the first three strata, forty-five villages are selected on the basis of probability proportional to size (PPS) of the number of households in the village. From those villages in the last strata ninety are selected, using a PPS design. A systematic random sample (SRS) of twenty households from each village in each strata is then selected, resulting in a total of 4,500 households. Within these households the head and married females of reproductive age are interviewed.

The sample design is summarized in Table 4.1.

Table 4.1 Summary of sample design

Strata	Villages (PPS)	Households per village (SRS)	Total households
Large	45	20	900
Medium	45	20	900
Small	45	20	900
None	90	20	1,800
TOTAL	225	80	4,500

Data Collection

The fieldwork for the study was conducted between June and November 1980. This period was longer than intended because the rainy season began earlier than usual and a large portion of the sample villages were flooded.

Two teams of interviewers were used, each including ten interviewers and two supervisors. Editing and checking of interview schedules were conducted in the field on the same day as the interview was conducted.

Operational Definitions of the Variables

The operational definitions of the variables are as follows:

1) Development program outputs
   a) size of an agricultural irrigation project, i.e. 'large,' 'medium' and 'small' as defined above under the section 'Agricultural Irrigation';

- b) length of time (in years) that an irrigation project has been in the village;
- c) participation of a household in the irrigation project, including making labor and capital contributions as well as using project outputs, scaled as 'none,' 'some,' 'moderate,' and 'high';
- d) number of years electricity has been available in the village;
- e) presence of a health station in a village;
- f) presence of a school in a village.

2) Socioeconomic status
   - a) landholding—amount of land owned by the household;
   - b) total household income;
   - c) males—employment in non-agricultural occupations;
   - d) females—employment in non-agricultural occupations and number of years of school completed.

3) Norms of family size
   - a) the total number of living children plus the additional number of children desired.

4) Intermediate variables
   - a) the current practice of family planning;
   - b) number of months of breastfeeding of the last child.

5) Fertility
   - a) the number of live births three years prior to the survey.

Results and Conclusions

Characteristics of Sample Villages and Households

Table 4.2 presents a profile of the sample villages by the size of the irrigation system in the villages. There is a higher proportion of villages electrified with 'large' systems than with either 'medium' or 'small' systems, or no system. The proportions of villages with roads show little difference between the size of irrigation systems. However, the proportions of villages with health stations and family planning centers is higher for irrigated than non-irrigated villages; and the proportions of villages with primary schools is highest for villages with a 'small' sized system.

Table 4.2 Proportions of sample villages with selected characteristics by size of irrigation system in the villages, 1979

Characteristics	Size of irrigation system			
	Large	Medium	Small	None
			%	
Electricity	48.6	31.6	33.3	17.6
Village road	94.7	89.7	92.3	94.6
Health station	20.0	30.0	29.0	17.7
Family planning center	72.7	80.6	30.0	10.0
Primary school	78.9	72.2	89.2	72.5
N =	(45)	(45)	(45)	(90)

Table 4.3 presents a summary of the variables utilized in the following analysis for households in villages with different sizes of irrigation systems. The proportions of males and females employed in non-agricultural occupations, and the mean monthly income of household heads is higher in villages with 'large' irrigation systems than in villages with either 'medium' or 'small' systems, or no system. Desired family size is lower, and the mean months of breastfeeding and proportions currently using contraception is higher among households from villages with 'large' than with 'medium' or 'small' systems, or no system. Finally, recent fertility is lower among households in villages with any size of irrigation system than in households with no system.

The remaining portion of this section is divided into two parts. The first part presents the results of multiple regression analyses of the effects of irrigation and other development indicators on male and female occupational status, and household income. The second part presents the results of multiple regression analyses which illustrate the relationships and links between the development programs, socioeconomic status, intermediate variables, and fertility. In each of these analyses selected village characteristics are utilized as well as household and couple characteristics. The village characteristics are assigned to the sample of couples selected from the village. For example, those couples living in villages with irrigation systems are assigned scores according to the size of the system in the village and those living in villages with no system are

Table 4.3 Socioeconomic and demographic characteristics of households by size of village irrigation system, 1979

Characteristics	Size of irrigation system			
	Large	Medium	Small	None
Proportion of males employed in non-agricultural occupations	11.8	1.0	9.4	7.0
Proportion of females employed in non-agricultural occupations	8.3	4.6	4.7	3.8
Mean monthly income of household head (00 Baht)	66.0	41.0	49.0	42.0
Mean desired family size	3.5	3.8	3.8	3.8
Mean number of months of breastfeeding of last child	19.7	17.1	15.1	18.2
Proportions currently using family planning	45.0	39.0	40.2	38.0
Mean number of births in past three years	0.40	0.38	0.41	0.43
N =	900	900	900	1800

assigned a score of zero. Similarly, household characteristics, such as household income, are also assigned to couples in the household.

Impacts of Irrigation on Male and Female Occupation and Household Income

As seen in Table 4.4, size and length of time of an irrigation project exert a significant positive effect on male employment in non-agricultural occupations net of the effects of village characteristics such as electrification, presence of a health station and a school; and household characteristics such as the size of landholdings and female education. Participation of a household in an irrigation project also shows a significant relationship with male non-agricultural occupation but the effect is to increase participation of males in agricultural occupations. The relative importance of the three indicators of irrigation in predicting the participation of males in agricultural occupations is about the same.

Table 4.4 Summary of multiple regression analyses of the effect of development indicators on socioeconomic factors

Independent variables	Male non-agricultural occupation	Female non-agricultural occupation	Household income
	Beta coefficients		
Size of irrigation project	0.04*	0.05*	0.10*
Length of time irrigation project in village	0.03*	0.00	0.04*
Participation in irrigation project	-0.03*	-0.04*	-0.14*
Village electrification (years)	0.06*	0.02	0.03*
Health station	0.07*	0.09*	0.00
School	0.02*	0.00	0.01
Landholding	-0.22*	-0.14*	0.03*
Female education	0.10*	0.11*	-0.01
Male non-agricultural occupation			0.08
Female non-agricultural occupation			0.08*
R^2 =	0.08	0.05	0.04
N = (4,500)			

*Significant at <0.05

Both size of an irrigation project and participation in a project show significant relationships with female employment in non-agricultural occupations. However, the effect of the former indicator of irrigation is to increase while the effect of the latter indicator is to decrease female employment in non-agricultural occupations.

Household income is affected significantly by all three indicators of irrigation. The effects are positive for the size and length of time of an irrigation project and negative for the household's participation in a project. Household income is also affected indirectly by irrigation as it operates through male and female non-agricultural occupations, which increases household income. These relationships are illustrated by the diagrams contained in Table 4.4. These diagrams are equivalent to path diagrams and present only the significant indirect relationships between variables. Dependent variables are included in columns and antecedent variables in rows. The presence of a beta coefficient for a row variable indicates that this variable was included in the regression equation for the column variable. Hence, all 'causally prior' variables in the path model that the column (dependent) variable was regressed on are represented by a coefficient with the row variable. To follow the significant indirect paths one simply begins with the row variables in the boxes and follows the arrow to each subsequent column variable. Thus, the indirect effect of the size of irrigation on household income through male non-agricultural occupations can be estimated by multiplying the beta coefficient, 0.04, shown against size of irrigation in column (1) and the beta coefficient, 0.08, shown against male non-agricultural occupation in column (3). (This format of presentation of the significant indirect paths between variables is also used in Table 4.5 of this study.)

The difference in the direction of relationship between the village-level indicators of irrigation and socioeconomic status, and the household-level indicator and status, is most probably due to the definition utilized for the household indicator. Household participation in an irrigation project was scaled on the basis of the household's contribution of labor and/or capital to an irrigation project as well as the actual utilization of the project outputs for agriculture. Therefore, households with comparatively 'higher participation' are those with members most involved in agricultural activities, which results in a negative relationship with non-agricultural occupation; and since household income increases with non-agricultural occupations, participation shows a negative relationship with income.

Finally, as stated in the conceptual framework, irrigation was expected to increase household income through an increase in farm production as a result of a more effective land use pattern and higher cropping intensity. A direct positive effect of irrigation upon

Table 4.5 Summary of multiple regression analyses of the effect of agricultural irrigation on fertility as it operates through effects on socioeconomic status and intermediate variables

Independent variables	Male non-agricultural occupation	Female non-agricultural occupation	Household income	Desired family size	Breastfeeding	Family planning	Fertility
		Beta coefficients					
Size of irrigation project	0.04*	0.05*	0.10*				
Length of time irrigation project in village	0.03*	0.00	0.04*				
Participation in irrigation project	-0.03*	-0.04*	-0.14*				
Village electrification (Yrs)	0.06*	0.02	0.03*				
Health station	0.07*	0.09*	0.00				
School	0.02	0.00	0.01				
Landholding	-0.22*	-0.14*	0.03*				
Female education	0.10*	0.11*	-0.01	-0.04*	-0.08*	0.08*	
Male agricultural occupation			0.08*	-0.05*	-0.09*	-0.02	
Female non-agricultural occupation			0.08*	-0.01	0.01	0.02	
Household income				0.02	0.01	-0.03	
Desired family size						-0.19*	
Breastfeeding							-0.33*
Family planning							-0.05*
Duration of marriage				0.64	-0.02	0.10*	-0.36*
R^2 =	0.08	0.05	0.04	0.42	0.02	0.05	0.30
N = (4,500)							

household income was found, and a portion of this effect was probably due to increased production of the larger farms. Support for this reasoning is suggested by the finding that landholdings in addition to being positively related to agricultural occupations were also positively related to household income. However, the effects of irrigation are not only to raise household income directly through increased productivity, but indirectly through its positive effect on employment in non-agricultural occupations; and it is these occupations which contribute to a higher household income.

Impacts of Irrigation on Fertility

The relationships between irrigation, socioeconomic status, intermediate variables, and fertility are illustrated in Table 4.5. Irrigation projects can affect fertility through intervening variables (indicators of socioeconomic status) which in turn affect fertility by changing demand for children and intermediate variables. Surprisingly, the effects of two intervening variables (female participation in non-agricultural occupation and household income) on desired family size and two intermediate variables (breastfeeding and the use of contraception) are not significant statistically. Thus, though the indicator of irrigation at the village level increased female participation in non-agricultural occupations and household income, irrigation does not affect fertility through these changes. There are, however, two patterns of linkages through which irrigation exerts a significant effect on fertility (see diagram in Table 4.5). The first is through male's non-agricultural occupation, desired family size, and family planning, which results in a negative effect on fertility by the village-level indicators and a positive effect on fertility by the household-level indicator. The second pattern is also through male's non-agricultural occupation but it works through a decrease in breastfeeding, which in contrast to the first pattern results in a positive effect on fertility by the village-level indicators and a negative effect on fertility by the household-level indicator.

It is clear from the findings of this study that the effects of irrigation on fertility tend to neutralize each other. Both the village-level indicators and the household-level indicator can have either positive or negative fertility effects, depending on the intermediate variables they are operating through. For example, although breastfeeding reduces fertility it is practiced less among wives of males employed in non-agricultural occupations, and it is participation in these occupations which is increased by irrigation at the village level. However, these occupations are also associated with lower norms of family size which increases the level of family planning practice, resulting in lower fertility.

These mixed effects of irrigation highlight the rather complex and diverse sociodemographic outcomes that may be expected of irrigation programs. These outcomes, however, must be interpreted in the light of the rather low magnitude of effects, as evidenced by the low beta coefficients found between irrigation, socioeconomic status and selected intermediate variables. This cautionary note must also be extended to the conclusions drawn regarding the working hypothesis of the study. The hypothesis that irrigation programs will affect fertility through changes in socioeconomic status and the intermediate variables has been supported within the limits referred to above, but the direction of the fertility effect depends on the intermediate variable focussed upon and the level (i.e. village or household) of the measure of irrigation utilized.

Reference

Royal Irrigation Department, 1979. *Irrigation Projects Completed up to 1978 and Under Construction in 1979*. Royal Thai Government, p. 31.

5 Female Employment, Occupational Setting and Fertility in a Philippine City

*Michael A. Costello and Marilou Palabrica-Costello**

Introduction

Any consideration of the impacts of development on fertility must take into account the role played by female labor force participation, particularly within Southeast Asia. Rates of economic growth in this region have been satisfactory over the past few decades, while fairly substantial patterns of declining fertility have also been noted. Since rates of female labor force participation in the region are also high, the possibility exists that these different factors are functionally interrelated. Implicit assumptions are often made to the effect that, first, economic development increases the proportion of gainfully employed women in the formal sector and in urban manufacturing establishments, and second, that this increase in employment leads to lower fertility.

The overall applicability of the first assumption to the Southeast Asian context still appears appropriate: industrial growth has been rapid in such countries as South Korea, Taiwan and Singapore, and women are often preferred for employment in textiles, electronics and food-processing industries. A trend towards increased labor force participation among women in general, and among married women in particular, is under way in many of the countries in Southeast Asia. The present study has thus been designed to shed further light on the assumption concerning the relationship between female employment patterns and their childbearing behavior. In particular, the applicability of the theory of role incompatibility to predict the effect of occupational settings on fertility is examined in the medium-sized Philippine city of Cagayan de Oro.

* Research Associates, Research Institute for Mindanao Culture, Xavier University, Cagayan do Oro City, Philippines.

Theoretical Background

Social scientists investigating the relationship between female employment and fertility have generally held that working women will bear fewer children than those who are not gainfully employed. For economists, this inverse relationship is the expected outcome of the increased opportunity costs that childbearing may bring for employed women; for example, income foregone by mothers who stay at home to take care of their young children, and such problems as decelerated career mobility or difficulties associated with re-entry into the labor market after childbirth. Overall, the negative effect of these costs on the demand for children is posited to outweigh any positive effect which might result from increases in household income due to the wife's salary.

Sociologists have also given a number of reasons for expecting an inverse relationship between female employment and fertility. Working wives may have greater exposure to sources of satisfaction—both monetary and non-monetary—other than those offered by the traditional female roles of wife and mother (Blake, 1965). Working women might feel a pressure to postpone or to curtail altogether further births if child care responsibilities entail a foregoing of these satisfactions. Employment has been associated with heightened levels of personality modernization (Inkeles & Smith, 1974) and household decision making power (Weller, 1968; Youssef, 1982), both of which might aid in the adoption of family planning. The access gained by working wives to non-domestic social networks could also generate increased knowledgeability and innovativeness with regard to fertility control techniques.

A particularly influential line of thought has been proposed by advocates of 'role incompatibility' theory (Stycos & Weller, 1967). According to this perspective, working mothers are likely to experience conflicting role demands, especially when their children are still young. Reduced commitments to either the occupational or the maternal role are seen as a likely response to this situation, for example, by working on only a part-time basis, by opting out of the labor market altogether, or by deciding to restrict future childbearing. When the latter alternative is chosen with some frequency, and when access to family planning techniques is sufficiently widespread as to make this a realistic choice, a general tendency for working women to bear fewer children should be noted.

According to role incompatibility theory the strength of the relationship between female employment status and fertility may be affected by the type of work roles open to women. Some jobs are more compatible with maternal roles than others, and women who work in these jobs (e.g., within their own homes or as self-employed women in sales and service occupations) have been found to exhibit fertility levels which are as high as those found among housewives (Jaffe & Azumi, 1960; Goldstein, 1972; and Bhattacharyya & Hayes, 1983). Women employed in such settings will in many cases be able to watch their children as they work or arrange their working hours so as to maximize the fit between occupational and familial responsibilities. Conversely, women who work far from their homes will experience a greater sense of role incompatibility than will those whose job is near to their place of residence, as will full-time workers compared to those employed on a part-time basis.

A review of empirical studies on this topic indicates that the relationship between female employment status and fertility within more developed nations is somewhat different from that within less developed nations. In the former setting most studies do show the expected pattern (see for example, Ridley, 1959 and Jones, 1981).

Findings from the less developed world are less uniform. Gross comparisons between working and non-working wives are often unable to find any significant fertility differential between these two groups (e.g., Stycos and Weller, 1967; Gurak and Kritz, 1982) and even analyses which have sought to distinguish between work settings with varying levels of role incompatibility have frequently failed to obtain the expected results (see, for example, Hein, 1982 for Mauritius; Mason & Palan, 1981 for Malaysia; and Stokes & Hsieh, 1983 for Taiwan). Researchers in the Philippines have also been generally unable to establish an inverse relationship between female employment status and fertility (see a review done by Herrin, 1980).

One way in which role incompatibility theory has attempted to deal with these negative findings is by pointing to differences in household structure between more or less developed countries. Access to potential mother surrogates is seen as working to reduce incompatibility between maternal and working roles, even in cases where the wife is employed on a full-time basis, far from her home, or in a formal-sector work setting. Indeed, these types of jobs are likely to facilitate the hiring of one or more domestic servants for childcare purposes, on the assumption that they offer higher wages than do the other types of gainful employment which have been more traditionally open to women. Extended kin living within the household may represent another childcare resource which can be tapped by working mothers, as can older children who are no longer enrolled in school. However, one of the few studies which have attempted to empirically quantify this dimension found that there was little or no influence of household compositional factors upon the strength of the work–fertility relationship in Malaysia (Mason & Palan, 1981).

One problem with role incompatibility theory which might account for these empirical failures lies in the fact that it has not paid adequate attention to the role played by proximate fertility determinants other than contraception. In particular, infant feeding practices have not been dealt with in most tests of this perspective. Adjustments in their maternal role by working mothers may include a decrease in their extent and duration of breastfeeding. Unless this change is accompanied by a compensating increase in the use of contraception, it will tend to increase fertility levels insofar as breastfeeding tends to have a natural contraceptive effect. Positive correlations between duration of breastfeeding and length of the birth interval have been found for a number of societies (Jain & Bongaarts, 1981), with the influence of this factor appearing to be especially important in settings with a low prevalence of contraceptive use (Potter, 1975; Bongaarts, 1983).

Another set of reasons for observing a lack of uniform relationship between employment and fertility in less developed countries is methodological in character. Model mis-specification and inadequate attempts to deal with the non-recursive nature of the relationship represent two major pitfalls along these lines. Another problem lies in the exceedingly diverse measures which have been used to quantify both employment status and fertility. Employment has been measured by pre-marital, post-marital, and current working status, or in other instances by the number of years since marriage spent working by the wife. Various measures of fertility which have been used include those that quantify both current and cumulative fertility, fertility desires, and even family planning use. In many cases, measures of current employment status have been correlated with cumulative fertility levels, thus raising the whole question of temporal priority on the part of the presumed causal variable.

The study design used in the present analysis has sought to avoid some of the shortcomings just noted. Gross contrasts between working and non-working women have been eschewed in favor of differences among three quite specific job settings which differ radically on the role incompatibility dimension but which are similar enough in social status so as to allow for meaningful comparisons. These are: low-skilled employees of a large pineapple-canning factory, self-employed market vendors, and women working as salaried employees of small-scale commercial establishments. A comparative sample of non-employed women (housewives) is also included in the analysis. Infant feeding practices have been carefully measured by the present study, and attention has been given to the problem of demonstrating temporal priority on the part of the employment status variable.

Based on role incompatibility theory, one would expect the factory operatives to have lower fertility than either the housewives or the other types of working women. Punctuality is strictly enforced in the company under observation, while frequent absences, as might be caused by sick children or other maternal responsibilities, are grounds for dismissal from the job. No company-run nursery exists on the premises and mothers employed therein are not allowed to bring their children to work. Thus, they must find someone to watch their young children during working hours. The overall effect would be that the demand for children among factory workers would be lower than that among the other three groups. The extent to which this gets translated into lower marital fertility, however, would depend upon what happens to the use of contraception and breastfeeding.

On the one hand, factory employment might be expected to accelerate the adoption of birth control techniques because women working within this setting have access to the company-sponsored health clinic, which offers family planning counselling services and supplies to company employees. Factory employment has also been reported to bring about increased levels of personality modernization (Inkeles & Smith, 1974), which should be related positively to family planning use.

On the other hand, women employed in the factory setting may be expected to experience greater difficulty in breastfeeding, due in large measure to the very problem of role incompatibility already discussed. Previous studies on this issue are not of one accord, but the general pattern would appear to be that employment status is correlated negatively with breastfeeding practices, most particularly for women employed far from their homes or in the formal sector (for a literature review, see Van Esterik & Greiner, 1981). Breastfeeding status, therefore, may represent an important intervening link which can operate to bring about a positive relationship between female employment and fertility.

The present study makes a comparison between the fertility patterns predicted by role incompatibility theory and those based on the three-way relationship between employment, infant feeding practices, and fertility. The former perspective hypothesizes that fertility levels should be lowest among factory employees, followed in order by women working within the informal sector (vendors and employees of small-scale establishments) and the housewife group; the latter hypothesizes that the relationship between occupational setting and fertility should be negligible or may even run in the *opposite* direction. Role incompatibility theory also posits a positive relationship between access to maternal surrogates and fertility, while the breastfeeding argument assumes that this relationship will be negligible.

Methodology

The Study Area

Cagayan de Oro is located on the northern coast of the island of Mindanao. The city functions chiefly as an administrative and commercial center for the surrounding region. A fair amount of manufacturing has located in or near the city, attracted chiefly by the availability of cheap electrical power from a nearby hydroelectric generating station. The oldest of these establishments is a large pineapple canning factory which was opened in 1929 and which now employs over 4,800 workers, a majority of whom are women.

As of 1980, Cagayan de Oro had about 225,000 inhabitants, making it the tenth largest city in the country. Between 1975 and 1980 the city grew by 6.59 percent per annum, a rate which was faster than all but three of the nation's sixty chartered cities. The population of the city is predominantly Roman Catholic.

Fertility rates in the region have historically been high, even for a developing country. The total fertility rate in the early 1960s was about 7.0 and the total marital fertility rate was nearly 11.0 (Madigan, 1972). A rather substantial fertility decline has taken place during the past decade, chiefly due to a trend towards delayed marriage, although signs of decline in marital fertility are also evident (Madigan & Costello, 1980). Use of family planning is now common among married couples, with the most popular methods being calendar rhythm, ligation, anovulant pills and withdrawal.

Sampling Methodology

For the factory employees, a sample of low-skilled ('base') workers was selected from company personnel files. Mapping and listing operations were conducted to select the other three sub-samples. For the housewives, the list consisted of all currently married non-employed women in Cagayan de Oro's *poblacion* (urban core). Vendors working within the four public markets in the city were also listed, as were married women employed by small scale manufacturing and commercial establishments throughout the city. This latter category included such enterprises as dressmaking shops, small stores, restaurants, and beauty parlors. Establishments employing fifty or more workers were excluded from the sample as no longer being small scale in nature. Women working in managerial or white collar jobs in these establishments were excluded from the sample.

For the factory, market vendor and housewife groups, 350 respondents were selected for interview. However, the number of married women employed in small scale establishments throughout the city did not prove large enough to allow for a sample of this size. Only 209 such cases were located, all of whom were interviewed. There were also two refusals, thus bringing the final sample size to 1,257 married women aged 20 to 44.

Interviews were conducted during February–April 1982. Replacements were randomly chosen for cases which had been incorrectly identified as being eligible for the survey during the initial listing operations. All data were edited and verified according to standard procedures. Further details on sampling procedures and field work may be found in the final project report (Costello & Palabrica-Costello, 1984).

Conceptual Framework

The conceptual framework used in this study is schematically shown in Figure 5.1. In this framework, women's employment status is a function of such background characteristics as her age and educational attainment and is assumed to affect her fertility-related attitudes and behavior through intervening and intermediate variables.

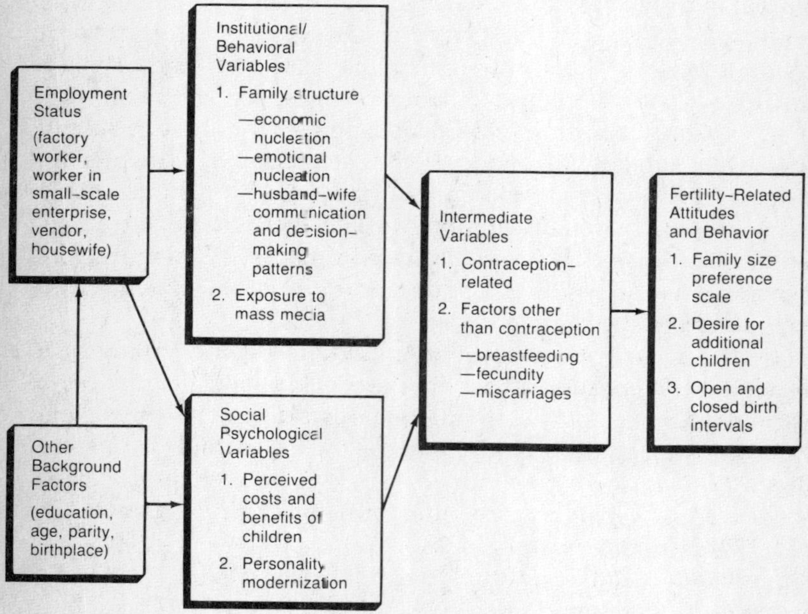

Figure 5.1 Conceptual framework of the study

A major methodological issue for the study concerns the problem of causality. In this framework work roles are viewed as one of the determinants of fertility-related attitudes and behavior, but the opposite may also be true. Women who have recently given birth to a child may be less likely to seek employment than those who have not. Even if such women were to look for a job, discrimination by potential employers or difficulties in finding childcare services could similarly work to reduce their chances of obtaining gainful employment. Among older women, past childbearing activities could influence current labor force participation rates. Women with large numbers of living children, for example, may feel a greater need to earn additional income for their families than would those with smaller families.

In the present study this issue has been dealt with by using data from a work history administered to all respondents in conjunction with two measures of current fertility (length of the open and closed birth intervals), and one measure of fertility desires. For the analysis of the two fertility measures, work status has been measured at the beginning of the respective birth interval, rather than at the date of interview, in order to insure that the employment status factor was measured at a point in time prior to the dependent variable. The two proximate fertility variables which have been shown to be of greatest importance in the Philippines are family planning use and breastfeeding practices (National Census and Statistics Office *et al.*, 1979). Particular emphasis was thus paid to these variables, though some attention was also given to differences among employment status categories in fecundity levels and miscarriage rates.

Intervening variables are classified into three broad categories: institutional, behavioral and social-psychological. Institutional/behavioral factors investigated in the preliminary analysis consisted of various family structure factors (interspousal communication and power relationships) and the use of the mass media, while the initial social-psychological factors included measures of the values and costs of childbearing, with particular emphasis upon the perceived economic and emotional benefits of children. Preliminary analyses of the data showed that most of these measures were not significantly related to employment status (Costello & Palabrica-Costello, 1984). However, two factors, personality modernization and media use, did show a significant relationship with employment status, and were thus included in the multivariate analysis of the fertility measures. As predicted, the first of these was found to be significantly higher among factory employees. This same group, however, scored lowest on the index of mass media use, with the housewives ranking highest in this regard.

Operational definitions of all variables used in the regression analysis are presented in Appendix 1.

Background variables most typically included in the multivariate analysis presented below were the respondent's birthplace (whether rural or urban), her education, age and parity, and an index of ownership of consumer durables. This latter variable was used to indicate the couple's economic status. In general, inter-occupational differences in these background variables were not large (See Table 5.1). Factory workers were better educated than the other three groups, with housewives ranking second in this regard. Vendors were about three years older, on the average, than respondents in the other three subsamples. This group had also given birth to more children and owned a larger number of consumer goods. Housewives had a somewhat earlier age at marriage than did working women, indicating a possible delaying effect of female employment upon age at marriage. No significant differences were found among the four groups in terms of rural-urban origins.

Table 5.1 Background information on sample respondents: percentages and means by occupational category, Cagayan de Oro City, Philippines, 1982

	Occupational Category			
Background Variable	Factory	Small scale	Vendor	Housewife
a) Birthplace (% born in a city)	26.9	27.3	35.1	33.1
b) Education (mean no. of years)	9.3	8.5	8.4	9.0
c) Average number of consumer goods owned	6.8	5.3	7.6	6.2
d) Average age (years) at interview	30.6	30.5	33.1	30.7
e) Average age at marriage (years)	22.3	22.3	21.2	21.0
f) Average duration of marriage (years)	8.3	8.2	11.9	9.7
g) Children ever born (mean)	3.0	2.8	4.3	3.5
Number of cases	350	209	348	350

Findings

The stepwise multiple regression analyses are done for the additional number of children desired, the length of the open birth interval, and two proximate fertility determinants—current use of family planning and average duration of breastfeeding in the last closed birth interval. The open birth interval, which refers to the duration (in months) between the birth of the last child and the interview, is used as an indicator of current fertility. To focus on more recent fertility, intervals longer than sixty months are excluded from the analysis. The regression coefficients for all variables included in the equations are not presented. We only present the regression coefficients for the dummy variables signifying the three occupational settings. In this analysis, the category of housewives is used as the reference group. The results of these regression analyses are shown in Tables 5.2 and 5.3.

In the stepwise regression approach used here, three occupational dummies are introduced at the first step, while background variables are brought in at the second step, intervening variables at the third step, and (for the analysis of the open birth interval) proximate determinants at the fourth step. Thus, the regression coefficients shown in the first column of Tables 5.2 and 5.3 measure the gross or total effect of each of the occupational settings in comparison with the value for housewives. The regression coefficients shown in the remaining columns measure the net effect of these occupational settings after controlling for the effect of variables introduced at each of the successive steps. The following discussion of these results is divided into four sections: desire for additional children, current fertility, use of family planning and breastfeeding.

Desire for Additional Children

When asked if they would like to give birth to one or more additional children, only a minority (37 percent) of the respondents answered in the affirmative. Surprisingly, women working in small scale industries (46 percent) and in the factory (42 percent) were somewhat more likely to desire another child than housewives (34 percent) or vendors (30 percent). However, there are no significant occupational differences in the average number of additional

Table 5.2: Regression coefficients (unstandardized) for occupational settings in regression analysis of indicators of fertility in Cagayan de Oro City, Philippines, 1982

Occupational setting	Desired number of future births**		
	Step 1	Step 2	Step 3
Factory	0.09	0.00	0.02
Small-scale	0.27*	0.14	0.14
Vendor	-0.05	0.10	0.10
Intercept	0.56	1.62	1.68
R^2	0.01	0.28	0.28
N	1256		

Occupational setting	Average open birth interval (months)‡			
	Step 1	Step 2	Step 3	Step 4
Factory	-4.07*	-4.40*	-3.45*	-2.40
Small-scale	-5.84*	-5.59*	-5.27*	-3.17
Vendor	0.09	-2.47	-2.17	-0.63
Intercept	22.16	17.69	11.99	2.70
R^2	0.02*	0.07*	0.08*	0.20*
N	723			

* $p < 0.05$

** Background variables added at Step 2 are place of birth, education, age, parity, ownership of modern objects and current pregnancy status; intervening variables added at Step 3 are media use and personality modernization.

‡ Women who have not given birth to any child, who were not occupying their present occupational status at the beginning of the birth interval, and whose open birth interval exceeded sixty-one months were excluded from the analysis. Background variables added at Step 2 are education, age at the beginning of the open birth interval, ownership of modern objects and parity; intervening variables added at Step 3 are media use and personality modernization; and proximate variables added at Step 4 are breastfeeding, use of contraception, miscarriages, and regularity of menstruation in the open birth interval.

Table 5.3: Regression coefficients (unstandardized) for occupational settings in regression analysis of current use of family planning and the duration of breastfeeding in Cagayan de Oro City, Philippines, 1982

Occupational setting	Current family planning use**		
	Step 1	Step 2	Step 3
Factory	1.9	3.6	0.9
Small-scale	-11.3*	-5.2	-3.8
Vendor	0.3	-3.6	-1.6
Intercept	68.2	53.9	69.0
R^2	0.01	0.08	0.18
N	(1015)		

Occupational setting	Average duration of breastfeeding (months) in the last closed birth interval‡		
	Step 1	Step 2	Step 3
Factory	-3.58*	-3.16*	-2.92*
Small-scale	-0.39	-0.38	-0.44
Vendor	-1.03	-1.41	-1.36
Intercept	6.49	10.32	11.03
R^2	0.05	0.10	0.11
N	(555)		

* $p < .05$

** Background variables added at Step 2 are place of birth, education, age, parity and ownership of modern objects; while intervening variables added at Step 3 are media use, personality modernization, and desire for additional children. Women who were currently pregnant, whose husbands were out of the country or who reported themselves as no longer able to bear a child (for reasons other than ligation or vasectomy) are excluded from the analysis.

‡ Except for desire for additional children, variables added at Steps 2 and 3 are the same as noted in **. Women with 0 or 1 parity and those not employed in the same occupation at the time of their last-but-one birth have been excluded from the analysis.

children desired once the effects of the background factors have been taken into account (see Table 5.2, top Panel, Column 2). Evidently, the higher fertility desires voiced by women employed in small scale industries or in the factory are largely due to the fact that they have as yet given birth to fewer children than the other respondents (see Table 5.1). As expected, the multiple regression results (not shown in Table 5.2), showed parity to be negatively associated with future fertility desires, as were the wife's age and her level of educational attainment. Current pregnancy status was also found to be significantly linked to the dependent variable, in this case positively.

Data on future fertility desires may be further used to test role incompatibility theory. This theory postulates that the impact of female employment status on fertility will be attenuated in settings where surrogate mother figures—such as domestic helpers or older extended kin—are readily available. Conversely, the presence of maternal surrogates in the households of working mothers should be linked positively to the desire for future births among these women, since conflicts between domestic and working roles are nonproblematic for this group.

Three indicators of the availability of child care to working mothers are available from the study. The first of these (HELPCHILD) is based on a survey question which asked the respondent whether she felt that she could find someone to help her take care of a baby, should she give birth in the near future. The remaining two are based on the inspection of data from the household record and reflect the presence in the household of a domestic servant (SERVANT) or an adult extended relative (EXTKIN).

Zero-order correlation coefficients between the number of additional children desired by employed women and each of the three household structural variables for the sub-sample of working women were positive, as expected (See Table 5.4).

Table 5.4 Household structural variables for working women

Variable	r
HELPCHILD	0.06 ($p < .10$)
SERVANT	0.02 (p = n.s.)
EXTKIN	0.07 ($p < .05$)

These results might be interpreted as providing modest support for role incompatibility theory since working women who have access to potential child assistance are more likely to desire one or more future births. Such an interpretation, however, is not accurate because the effects of these three household structural variables were uniformly reduced and none of the partial regression coefficients remained statistically significant when the background variables were used as controls in a multiple regression analysis.

Current Fertility

In the present study, current fertility is measured by the open birth interval; thus, women who had not given birth to at least one child were excluded from this analysis. In order to establish temporal priority on the part of the occupational factor, women who were not employed in their current occupational category (or housewives who *were* gainfully employed) at the beginning of this interval were also excluded.

Contrary to the predictions of role incompatibility theory, women working in the factory and in small scale establishments were found to have shorter open birth intervals (or higher recent marital fertility) than vendors and housewives (see Table 5.2, Panel 2, Column 1). These occupational differences remained significant even after controlling for the effects of the background and intervening social-psychological variables. Interoccupational differences in the length of the open birth interval, however, do not remain significant after controlling for the effects of the proximate variables added at Step 4 (Table 2, Panel 2, Column 4). Thus, these observed occupational differences in current marital fertility appear to be the function of the proximate fertility variables, which are examined below.

Family Planning Practice

The use of family planning was found to be fairly widespread among the sampled respondents. About three out of every four eligible women (76.4 percent) reported that they had ever used a family planning method, while more than two-thirds (67.8 percent) reported themselves as being current users. These rather high prevalence levels are attributable in part to a widespread use of natural family planning methods (about 40 percent of the current users) which resulted from the detailed probes used in the study to inquire about the use of such techniques (rhythm, withdrawal, abstinence). Another reason for these high prevalence rates lies in the fact that women who were currently pregnant, whose husband was out of the country, or who reported themselves as no longer able to bear a child (for reasons other than ligation or vasectomy) were treated as ineligible in this tabulation. Inclusion of these women in the denominator reduces the percentage of ever and current users to 71.2 and 60.9 percent, respectively.

Inter-occupational differences in ever use, current use and type of family planning method currently used do not give strong support for the idea that working women in general, or factory employees in particular, are more prone to adopt family planning than non-employed wives. Indeed, housewives tend to rank somewhat higher on both the 'ever use' and 'current use' measures than do working women. The use of family planning methods is lowest among small scale employees. Factory workers rank highest on both ever use and current use, but the differences between women in this group and the market vendor and housewife sub-samples are negligible. Also, this group is more likely than the other three groups to be using such less effective techniques as calendar rhythm, condom, or withdrawal.

The low use of contraception among small scale employees does not remain significant statistically after controlling for the effects of background factors and intervening factors (see Table 5.3, Panel 1, Columns 2 and 3). There is, however, a significant interaction between job setting, parity and family planning use which had been identified in a preliminary analysis of the data (Costello & Palabrica-Costello, 1983). Interaction terms incorporating this effect were thus included at the fourth step of the multiple regression model of current family planning use (results not shown here). The coefficients for these terms were uniformly positive (most strongly so for factory workers), thus indicating that employment may only have the effect of increasing family planning use among high parity women. This point may be illustrated by data on the percentage of current users, by parity and occupational setting, as shown in Table 5.5. Among the high parity respondents, all three groups of

Table 5.5 Percentage of current contraceptive users, by parity and occupational setting

Occupational setting	Low parity (0-4 children)	High parity (5+ children)
Factory	64.4	92.1
Small Scale and Vendor	58.7	76.2
Housewife	69.3	70.6

women are found to be more likely to be current users of family planning methods. Among low parity women, housewives are most likely to be using some methods of family planning.

Breastfeeding

The proportion of women in our Cagayan de Oro sample who have decided not to breastfeed is high. Fully 39 percent of the eligible respondents did not breastfeed their second-to-last born child, while an even larger proportion (43 percent) did not use breastfeeding in the open birth interval. Comparable figures from the World Fertility Survey for the country as a whole stood at 14 and 15 percent in 1978 (National Census and Statistics Office, 1979). This differential is no doubt due largely to the fact that our sample is restricted to urban women, a majority of whom were reasonably well educated and gainfully employed at the time when these births occurred. The difference cannot be a function of differently worded questions since the survey items on breastfeeding which were employed in the present study were taken from the WFS module.

Mean lengths of breastfeeding were 5.0 and 4.3 months, respectively, for the closed and open birth intervals. Again, these averages are quite low, in comparison to both national and international figures.

Data on inter-occupational differences in breastfeeding practices are available for both the closed and open birth intervals. The latter measure, however, is subject to the problem of 'censored' observations in so far as some respondents were still breastfeeding at the time of the survey. This makes it impossible to assign estimates of the ultimate duration of breastfeeding for these cases. Greater attention will thus be accorded in this section to data from the closed birth interval, although findings for the most recently born child will also be briefly reviewed.

Mean durations of breastfeeding during the closed birth interval show a clear tendency for factory employees to be breastfeeding their newborn infants for shorter lengths of time. On the average, this group breastfed for only 2.9 months, as compared to 5.4 months for the combined small scale/vendor sub-sample and 6.6 months for the housewives.

Further insight into this issue is gained from results of a multiple regression analysis of breastfeeding duration. Factory workers clearly nurse their children for shorter intervals even after controlling for the effects of background and intervening variables (see Table 5.3, Panel 2, Columns 2 and 3). On the average, this group breastfed for about three fewer months than the housewives, net of the various control factors. Small scale employees and vendors also exhibited shorter durations, although the differences between these groups and the housewives were not large enough to attain statistical significance.

Data on the proportion of women who chose to breastfeed their most recently born child provide further support for the above findings. About 71 percent of the housewives chose this option, as compared to 57 percent of the combined small-scale/vendor category and only 42 percent of the factory workers. A regression analysis of this variable again showed this differential to persist strongly ($p < 0.001$ for the factory dummy), even after controlling for the effects of background and intervening variables. Overall, then, there appears to be strong evidence that employment in formal-sector occupations, such as a large-scale factory, is not compatible with the practice of breastfeeding.

Summary and Conclusions

Overall findings from this study failed to provide much confirmation for the theory of role incompatibility. Fertility was not found to be linked either negatively with working roles which were highly incompatible with domestic responsibilities or to be correlated positively with the presence of potential mother surrogates among employed respondents. Family planning use also showed no significant relation to occupational setting, except for the special case of high-parity women. In contrast, the major hypotheses concerning the role of breastfeeding have been confirmed. Results from both the open and closed birth intervals provide reasonably clear evidence that factory employment in Cagayan de Oro is linked positively, and not inversely, with current levels of marital fertility. It appears that a major reason for this finding lies in the decreased ability of working women—especially those employed in the factory setting—to breastfeed their offspring. Use of family planning represents another means by which the birth interval may be extended, but, in this study at least, the expected advantage of working women in this regard is not large enough to offset the effect of the infant feeding factor.

A few qualifications must be noted before generalizing the results of this study. In the first place, our findings apply only to a single, medium-sized city in the Philippines. Job-linked pressures towards fertility control might well be greater in larger cities, where journeys to work are more time-consuming and domestic servants most costly to maintain. Secondly, our findings leave open the possibility that female employment can have a delaying effect upon marriage, thus reducing overall fertility rates, even while marital fertility remains unchanged. Data from this study on the mean age at marriage among the four groups seem to imply this, as do results from national-level surveys in the Philippines (cf. Smith, 1978). Third, the significant interaction effect involving occupation, parity, and current family planning use also points to the possibility that employment may be negatively related to current marital fertility, but only when certain other factors, such as the economic problems generated by a relatively large family size, are present.

As noted in our literature review, empirical verification of the hypothetically inverse relationship between female employment and fertility has frequently not been obtained in the less developed world. An important implication of the present study thus lies in its identification of an intervening factor (infant feeding practices) which might be able to account for these reversals from the expected pattern. To date, most analyses of the relationship between women's work and fertility have failed to take this variable into account. Statistical models from these studies may thus be seriously mis-specified, with one likely result being biased estimates of the employment status coefficients. It is recommended that this over-sight be avoided in further analytic studies, and that action-oriented research be undertaken to determine ways by which greater use of breastfeeding can be encouraged among urban working women.

In terms of theory building, the study holds implications for the development-fertility issues raised at its outset. The process of economic modernization, it would seem, cannot always be expected to bring a trend towards reduced fertility in its wake. As Frank Lorimer (1954) noted over thirty years ago, there are certain traditional practices—in this case, prolonged breastfeeding—which may operate to keep birth rates below their biological maximum. Developmental trends which undermine these practices may thus be unable to stimulate a process of declining fertility; indeed, the opposite may sometimes prove to be the case (see Nag, 1980, for a similar effect of modernization on fertility).

A further specification of the conditions under which the role incompatibility theory operates would also seem necessary. In settings where breastfeeding levels are an important factor in regulating fertility levels, either because contraception is not widely practiced or (the Philippine case) because family planning use is fairly widespread but the less effective methods are commonly employed, incompatibility between maternal and occupational roles may not always decrease fertility. This would be particularly true in situations (again, as exemplified by the Philippine case) in which breast milk substitutes are readily available, thus making viable the option of deciding not to breastfeed one's baby. Our results, which are based on a sample of *low-skilled* working women, also raise the possibility that role incompatibility theory only applies among more highly skilled women workers, such as those in white collar occupations, where salaries and educational levels may be expected to be higher.

Disaggregation of the employment status variable has indicated that the constraints against breastfeeding seem to be particularly strong in the factory setting. Indeed, less than half of the factory respondents even *attempted* to nurse their most recent baby, a figure which is exceptionally low for a low-income, tropical setting such as Cagayan de Oro. Reports from other observers indicate a number of plausible reasons for this. Female factory laborers in the Philippines are not only prevented by prevailing management policies from bringing their babies to work with them, but they may also encounter difficulties in hand-expressing their milk during working hours. In some factories at the Bataan Export Processing Zone, for example, low skilled workers are not allowed to use

Zone, for example, low skilled workers are not allowed to use company rest rooms during these periods (Tañedo, 1983). Similarly, lunch breaks at the factory analyzed in the present study are short, while shifts in work schedules are frequently required. During peak canning seasons overtime work will be heavy, while at other times temporary layoffs are the norm. Night work is rotated on a regular basis, so that feeding schedules established for one week would have to be completely altered by the next. Faced with this situation, it is no wonder that so few factory workers have taken up the practice of breastfeeding.

These findings point to a need for structural changes in the jobs of working mothers. Campaigns to socialize young mothers into the advantages and techniques of breastfeeding will no doubt be of some help, but these cannot be expected to have much influence when conditions in the work situation itself actively discourage this type of infant feeding. Company-based childcare facilities would represent one such change, along with provisions for periodic work breaks for the purpose of breastfeeding, as incorporated within a larger program of maternity benefits. Statutes requiring benefits similar to these were formerly found in the Philippines, but have since been repealed, ostensibly because they led to sex discrimination in hiring practices. Whether this is in fact the case is open to debate, however, since recent social science research indicates that there is strong management preference for female employees in assembly line-type jobs in a number of industries (Aganon and Aganon, 1980). A more likely reason is, as Savani (1980, p. 87) has observed, that 'the lack of day care centers and nurseries, together with the absence of legal provisions to protect mothers, is to some extent a reflection of the low priority granted by governments to the problems encountered by women.'

References

Aganon, Virgilio, & Aganon, Maria, 1980. *A Study of Women Workers in Women-Dominated Manufacturing Establishments in Metro Manila*. Quezon City: Institute of Philippine Culture, Ateneo de Manila.

Bhattacharyya, Amit K. & Hayes, Adrian C, 1983. 'Cottage Industry and Fertility in West Bengal, India.' Paper presented at the 52nd Annual Meeting of the Population Association of America, Pittsburgh, 14–16 April.

Blake, Judith, 1965. 'Demographic Science and the Re-direction of Population Policy.' *Journal of Chronic Diseases*, **18**, pp.1181–200.

Bongaarts, John, 1983. 'The Proximate Determinants of Natural Fertility.' Pp.103-38 in Rodolfo A. Bulatao and Ronald D. Lee (eds.), *Determinants of Fertility in Developing Countries, Volume 1. Supply and Demand for Children*. New York: Academic Press.

Costello, Michael A., & Palabrica-Costello, Marilou, 1983. 'Female Employment, Occupational Setting and Family Planning Use in a Philippine City.' *Discussion Paper No. 3*, Cagayan de Oro City, Research Institute for Mindanao Culture.

Costello, Michael A., & Palabrica-Costello, Marilou, 1984. *Female Employment, Occupational Setting and Fertility in a Philippine City*. Cagayan de Oro, Research Institute for Mindanao Culture.

Goldstein, Sidney, 1972. 'The Influence of Labour Force Participation and Education on Fertility in Thailand.' *Population Studies*, **26**, pp.419–36.

Gurak, Douglas T., & Kritz, Mary M., 1982. 'Female Employment and Fertility in the Dominican Republic: A Dynamic Perspective.' *American Sociological Review*, **47**, pp.810–18.

Hein, C., 1982. 'Factory Employment, Marriage and Fertility: The Case of Mauritian Women.' *Working Paper No. 118*, Population and Labour Policies Programme. Geneva, World Employment Programme, International Labour Office.

Herrin, Alexandro N., 1980. *Population and Development Research in the Philippines: A Survey*. Report prepared for the Philippine Institute for Development Studies. Quezon City, School of Economics, University of the Philippines.

Inkeles, Alex & Smith, David H., 1974. *Becoming Modern: Individual Change in Six Developing Countries*. Cambridge: Harvard University Press.

Jaffe, A. J., & Azumi, K., 1980. 'The Birth Rate and Cottage Industries in Underdeveloped Countries.' *Economic Development and Cultural Change*, **9**, (October), pp.52–63.

Jain, Anrudh K., & Bongaarts, John, 1981. 'Breastfeeding Patterns, Correlates and Fertility Effects.' *Studies in Family Planning*, **12**, pp.79–99.

Jones, Elise F., 1981. 'The Impact of Women's Employment on Marital Fertility in the U.S., 1970–75.' *Population Studies*, **35**, pp.161-73.

Lorimer, Frank, 1954. 'General Theory.' pp.13–51 in F. Lorimer (ed.), *Culture and Human Fertility*, Part 1. Paris, UNESCO.

Madigan, Francis C., 1972. *Birth and Death in Cagayan de Oro: Population Dynamics in a Medium-Sized Philippine City*. Quezon City, Ateneo University Press.

Madigan, Francis C., & Costello, Michael A., 1980. 'The Area Fertility Studies of 1977 and 1978.' pp. 107–27 in Tito A. Mijares (ed.), *Proceedings of the National Seminar on the 1978 Republic of the Philippines*

Fertility Survey. Manila, National Census and Statistics Office.

Mason, Karen Oppenheim, & Palan, V. T., 1981. 'Female Employment and Fertility in Peninsular Malaysia: The Maternal Role Incompatibility Hypothesis Reconsidered.' *Demography*, **18**, pp.549–76.

Nag, Moni., 1980. 'How Modernization Can Also Increase Fertility.' *Current Anthropology*, **21**, pp.571–80.

National Census and Statistics Office, Republic of the Philippines, *et al.*, 1979. *World Fertility Survey/Republic of the Philippines Fertility Survey, 1978. First Report*. Manila, National Census and Statistics Office of the Philippines.

Potter, Robert G., 1975. 'Changes of Natural Fertility and Contraceptive Equivalents.' *Social Forces*, **54**, pp.36–51.

Ridley, Jeanne Clare. 1959. 'Number of Children Expected in Relation to Non-familial Activities of the Wife.' *The Milbank Memorial Fund Quarterly*, **37**, pp.277–96.

Savani, M., 1980. 'Yes to Breastfeeding, But . . . How?' *Assignment Children* **49/50**, pp.81–7.

Smith, Peter C., 1978. 'Trends and Differentials in Nuptiality'. pp.136– 59 in Mercedes B. Conception (ed.), *Population of the Philippines*. Bangkok, Economic and Social Commission for Asia and the Pacific.

Stokes, C. Shannon & Hsieh, Yeu-Sheng, 1983. 'Female Employment and Reproductive Behavior in Taiwan, 1980.' *Demography*, **20**, pp.313–32.

Stycos, J. Mayonne, & Weller, Robert H., 1967. 'Female Working Roles and Fertility.' *Demography*, **4**, pp.210–17.

Tañedo, Rochit I., 1983. 'It's the Women Who are Making the Bataan EPZ Flourish.' *Philippine Panorama*, **12**, (19), pp.4–8.

Weller, Robert H., 1968. 'The Employment of Wives, Role Incompatibility and Fertility: A Study Among Lower- and Middle-class residents of San Juan, Puerto Rico.' *The Milbank Memorial Fund Quarterly*, **45**, pp.507–27.

Youssef, Nadia H., 1982. 'The Interrelationships Between the Division of Labour in the Household, Women's Roles, and Their Impact on Fertility.' pp.173–201 in Richard Anker, Mayra Buvinic, & Nadia H. Youssef (eds.), *Women's Roles and Population Trends in the Third World*. London, Croom Helm.

Van Esterik, Perry, and Greiner, Ted, 1981. 'Breastfeeding and Women's Work: Constraints and Opportunities.' *Studies in Family Planning*, **12**, pp.184–97.

Appendix 1: Definition of Study Variables

Variable	*Definition*
AGE	Age (in years) of the respondent as of the survey date.
AGECBI	Age (in years) of the respondent at the beginning of the closed birth interval.
AGEOBI	Age (in years) of the respondent at the beginning of the open birth interval.
BFCBI	Duration of breastfeeding (in months) during the closed birth interval. Women who did not breastfeed scored as '0'.
BFOBI	Use of breastfeeding during the open birth interval. Dummy variable, scored as '1' for women who breastfed their last child.
BIRTH	Birthplace of the respondent. Dummy variable scored as '1' for women born in a rural setting. Births which occurred within a chartered city were defined as urban; all others as rural.
ED	Educational attainment of the respondent (highest grade of formal schooling completed).
EXTKIN	Presence of adult extended relatives within the household of the respondent. Dummy variable scored as '1' if at least one such relative (aged 15 or over) was present.
FACTORY	Employment within the factory setting. Dummy variable scored as '1' if the respondent worked in the factory.
FPCBI	Use of family planning during the closed birth interval. Dummy variable scored as '1' if family planning was ever used during this interval.
FPOBI	Use of family planning during the open birth interval.
HELPCHILD	Opinion as to whether or not childcare help could be obtained for another baby. Dummy variable scored as '1' if the respondent asserted that such help would be available.
INTERF	Interaction term between parity and the dummy variable for factory employment.
INTERS	Interaction term between parity and the dummy variable for small scale employment.
INTERV	Interaction term between parity and the dummy variable for employment as a market vendor.
MEDIA	Score on a summary index of mass media use (20-point scale). The index was formed by summing responses to

items on newspaper reading, movie-going, and use of television and radio.

MENSREG — Regularity of respondent's menstrual periods. Dummy variable scored as '1' if the respondent's menstrual periods came 'regularly,' at the interval of once a month. Women with irregular periods, or those with periods which regularly come at intervals extending beyond one month, scored as '0'.

MISCBI — Number of miscarriages which occurred during the closed birth interval.

MISOBI — Number of miscarriages which occurred during the open birth interval.

MODERN — Score on a summary index of personality modernization (14-point scale). The index used was the 'short form' (OM-12) of the personality modernization index, as originally developed by Inkeles and Smith (1974, pp. 348–51).

OWNCG — Score on a summary index of ownership of consumer goods (16-point scale). Items on the scale included ownership of an umbrella, flashlight, clock/watch, radio, camera, aparador (dresser), bed with a mattress, sala set (living room furniture), sewing machine, electric iron, electric/gas stove, television, stereo, refrigerator, air conditioner and automobile/truck.

PARITY — Number of children ever born alive to the respondent, in this and all previous marriages.

PREGNOW — Current pregnancy status of the respondent. Dummy variable scored as '1' if respondent was pregnant as of the survey date. (Women who were not sure of their pregnancy status were considered as not pregnant.)

SERVANT — Presence of a servant within the household. Dummy variable scored as '1' if at least one servant was present.

SS — Employment within the setting of a small scale manufacturing or commercial establishment. Establishments employing fifty or more persons considered as no longer small scale in nature. Dummy variable scored as '1' if the respondent worked in such an establishment.

VENDOR — Employment as a vendor in one of the city's four public markets. Dummy variable scored as '1' if the respondent was a market vendor.

6 Child Labour, Schooling and Fertility in Rural Karnataka, South India

*Ramesh Kanbargi and P. M. Kulkarni**

Introduction

Despite considerable decline in mortality and substantial inputs from development and family planning programmes, high fertility persists in many of the less developed countries. One response to this problem has been the proliferation of research and debate on the economic value of children in peasant societies during the last decade. However, child labour, one aspect of that value and in many societies the chief value, has received disproportionate attention in the population literature. A number of studies, though, support the hypothesis about the pronatalistic effect of child labour, ignore or pay inadequate attention to the role of child schooling. This study investigates the relationships between child labour, child schooling and fertility in a sample of villages in South India.

The Problem and Objectives

Some empirical results tend to support the hypothesis that economic value of children is associated with higher fertility in the less developed countries. An analysis of cross-sectional data of several countries found a significant positive correlation between the labour force participation rate of children and fertility, and concluded that an economic structure where child labour plays an important role is conducive to high fertility (Kasarada, 1971). Several econometric analyses based on data from Egypt (Schultz, 1970), Chile (Davanzo, 1972), Thailand (Maurer, Ralajazak & Schultz, 1973) and the Philippines (Harman, 1970) also found evidence of a positive correlation between the child labour force

* Population Research Centre, Institute for Social and Economic Change, Bangalore, India

participation rate and fertility; and another study in the Philippines applying a household production framework to micro data concluded that 'an increase in the value of child time has a significant positive effect on the completed fertility of households' (Rosenzweig, 1978).

A more in-depth analysis of child labour has been conducted in the villages of Java and Nepal (Nag, White & Peet, 1978), Bangladesh (Cain, 1977; Caldwell, 1979), and Malaysia (De Tray, 1983). These studies show that children of both sexes put in long hours of work and contribute substantially to their family labour needs. Some have even argued that in the given context having large numbers of children is an economically rational proposition.

Similar observations are made for India although no in-depth investigation has been conducted to collect detailed information on work-input of children. An econometric analysis of district-level data from the 1961 census found significant positive relationships between wage rates of children and birth-rates, and significant negative correlations between wage rates of children and gender-specific school enrolment rates (Rosenzweig, 1977). Mamdani (1972), based on his observations on the social structure of Manpur village in Punjab, argued forcefully that, for most groups, high rather than low fertility would constitute 'rational' economic behaviour because children perform a variety of tasks beneficial to their parents. Nadkarni, while arguing that poor households in the Marathwada region of Maharashtra have no surplus labour, found that children in those households do considerable work both inside and outside the home (Nadkarni, 1976). A more recent study conducted in six villages of Karnataka found that the burden of collecting firewood for the family falls on the children, and that children are removed from school to carry out this activity which is crucial for the survival of the family (Reddy, 1980).

Vlassoff's study in rural Maharashtra, however, reports findings which contradict the findings of the studies mentioned above. He concludes that 'The common sense view of young children as poor man's capital is not accurate and clearly in the surveyed area economic costs outweighed the benefits of sons (and *a fortiori* of daughters) up to age sixteen' (Vlassoff, 1979).

Although several in-depth studies have been conducted on the economic contribution of children in less developed countries some important questions have remained unanswered. If child labour is an important determinant of fertility behaviour it is essential to know, from a policy point of view, how child labour can be reduced to a lower level. Banning child labour may not be a practical suggestion in a subsistence economy where families try to utilize the labour of most of their members. The only viable solution seems to be in encouraging the children to attend school. However, if this policy were implemented, how much child labour would it reduce? Thus far, studies that have collected detailed data on work input of children only present the average time spent in school and do not compare the work input of school-going and non-school-going children. Further, the few studies on work input of children have either ignored or insufficiently investigated the role of such key variables as schooling, size of landholdings, number of siblings, and family type (nuclear or joint, etc.) in child labour fertility relationships (see, for example, Nag *et al.*, 1978; and Mamdani, 1972).

Taking into consideration the problems and shortcomings of previous research pointed out above, the objectives of the present study on the relationship between child labour, schooling and fertility in India are:

— to assess the actual work input of children;
— to examine the relationship between child labour and schooling and their social, economic and demographic determinants; and
— to determine the effect of child labour and school attendance on the reproductive behaviour of the population.

The Setting

The study was conducted in Karnataka State, which ranks second only to the State of Andhra Pradesh in the rate of prevalence of child labour. Karnataka (formerly known as Mysore) is the eighth largest state in India, with a population of 37 million in 1981. The population growth rate has been around 2 percent per annum for the last three decades. The crude birth-rate which was nearly 40 per thousand in the 1950s and 60s has declined to about 30 at the beginning of the 1980s. The expectation of life at birth is estimated to be in the range of 50–55 years for both males and females.

Methodology

Analytical Model

The general analytical model presented in Figure 6.1 is based on the assumption that child labour and child schooling affect each other; each is affected by a set of exogenous factors, and both indirectly affect their parents' desire for children and actual fertility through selected intermediate variables. This model is tested at the micro level where the individual is the unit of analysis. A list of all the variables and their operational definitions is presented in a later section.

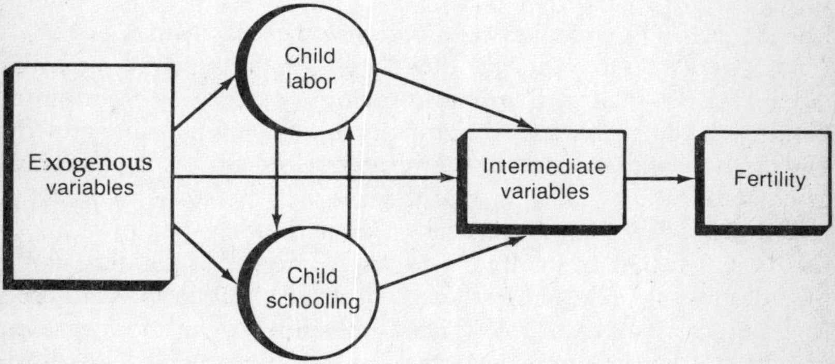

Figure 6.1 General analytical model for analysis

Two social-psychological variables, 'aspiration level' and 'opportunity consciousness,' are utilized as exogenous variables. The rationale for expecting the effect of these variables upon child labour and schooling requires explanation. We expect that parents from the lower socioeconomic strata who send their children to school will have a high 'aspiration level,' and believe that educating their children is one of the major ways of advancing in the socioeconomic hierarchy. It is customary to correlate educational achievement of children with their own aspirations. But in a patriarchal society it is the father who generally makes the decisions regarding the schooling of his children. Therefore, it is his aspiration level that acts as the decisive factor, at least in the early stage of child schooling.

'Opportunity consciousness' is intimately related to, but goes beyond 'aspiration level.' A person who aspires to a better quality of life would be expected to utilize available opportunities to achieve that goal. Such a person would be well-informed about the developmental programmes aimed at improving the socioeconomic conditions of the population. Thus, the aspiration level refers to a mental disposition for reaching certain sets of goals while opportunity consciousness represents the acquired knowledge and information which would aid in reaching the goals.

Sample Design

The districts of Karnataka State were stratified on the basis of 1971 census data into two groups: those with a high incidence of child labour (HCLDs) located primarily in the northern and southern plains, which are characterized by a low rate of literacy, low rainfall and cultivation of dry crops, and those districts with a low incidence of child labour (LCLDs) located primarily in the coastal and hilly areas, characterized by relatively higher literacy, heavy rainfall, paddy cultivation and coffee, acrenut, and coconut plantations.

The sample is selected from each of these strata in three stages. In the first stage, fifteen Taluks (an administrative unit smaller than a district; a district contains several Taluks), nine from HCLDs and six from LCLDs, were selected with probability proportional to size. In the second stage three villages were selected from each of the Taluks, again by probability proportional to size. In the final stage selection of the households from these villages was done systematically. Sample sizes were determined such that the household sample became self-weighting within each strata, and the weights almost identical in the two strata. One in every two households selected in the sample villages was chosen for collecting data on work input of children and adults.

Data on 2,070 households from forty-five villages were obtained from a household survey, and work input information was collected from twelve monthly visits from 1,035 of these households. Data for the micro level were collected from 1,095 currently married men aged 20–49 years with at least one surviving child aged 5–14 years. Data on work activity were collected for all children aged 5–14 years. A summary of the sample size is provided in Table 6.1.

Table 6.1 Summary of household sample size

	HCLD districts	LCLD districts	Total
No. of Taluks	9	6	15
No. of villages	27	18	45
No. of households	1,242	828	2,070
No. of households for work input data	621	414	1,035
No. of currently married men	657	438	1,095
No. of children aged 5–14 years for which work activity data are available	420	308	728

Data Collection

The data on work input of children 5–14, adult males aged 15–34, and adult females aged 15–49 were collected from each of the households sampled for this purpose through monthly visits for one year. The work activities performed by all the eligible persons on the previous day were recorded using a preconstructed itemized activity sheet which was prepared after extensive observation in each of the sample villages. Three field supervisors constantly assessed the data collected by checking the itemized activity sheet and revisiting sample households for spot verification. Principal investigators often paid surprise visits to the field to further verify the data.

A household survey was conducted at the end of the survey of work-input data, and background information on socioeconomic and demographic variables was collected. During this survey each eligible male (currently married with at least one surviving child aged 5–14) was administered an additional questionnaire to elicit information on his opportunity consciousness, aspiration level, contraception, and ideal family size.

A separate schedule was used to collect information on several variables at the village level from government officials such as village accountants, school headmasters, and agricultural extension officers.

Operational Definitions of Variables

The variables and their definitions used in this analysis are as follows:

1. Ideal family size—	the total number of children considered ideal.
2. Contraceptive practice—	the current use of contraception.
3. Female work input—	the number of hours per day in all work activities.
4. Livestock (cattle)—	the number of heads of cattle owned by the household.
5. Rainfall—	the average annual rainfall in mm. during 1971–81 in the village (or nearest weather station).
6. Landholding—	the total land cultivated by the household in acres.
7. Caste—	membership in dominant caste (Lingayat, Vokkaliga, Bunt, Brahmin), scheduled caste or tribe (SC)
8. Family type—	membership in nuclear or non-nuclear family.
9. Aspiration level—	an index computed from responses to questions on the respondent's aspirations about his children.
10. Opportunity consciousness—	an index computed from responses to questions on the respondent's awareness of various opportunities.
11. Education of father—	the number of years of school the father has completed.
12. School accessibility—	the presence of a middle school (fifth grade and above) in the village.

13. Past mortality experience— the percentage of siblings of the father surviving at the time of survey.
14. Presence of younger children— the number of children in the 0–4 age group.
15. Living children— the total number of children alive.
16. Sex composition of children— the ratio of living sons to living children.
17. Age of the youngest child— the age of the youngest living child in months.

Statistical Technique

The statistical technique utilized to test the model is multiple regression analysis. The model is not fully recursive because of the reciprocal relationship between child labour and schooling, and therefore ordinary least squares techniques cannot be employed to obtain regression coefficients. Two types of analysis are undertaken. In one analysis, the coefficients are obtained by a two-stage least squares method where the estimates from the reduced form of equations are substituted for the endogenous variables (See Duncan, 1975). In the first stage, equations for child labour and schooling are obtained from the reduced forms. These estimates are then used in the second stage as independent variables along with the relevant exogenous variables in the equations. In the second analysis, the child schooling variable is split into two variables: whether or not the child goes to school and the time spent in school. The dichotomous child schoolgoing variable is used as antecedent variable to both child labour and time spent in school. Child labour, in this analysis, is assumed to affect time spent in school, on the assumption that the demand for child labour will reduce the time spent by him/her in school.

Cross tabulations have been employed to illustrate the pattern of schoolgoing and work input by background variables.

In a substantial number of cases either no information was available on child work activities or if information was available it was only for one or two months. Hence, it was decided to restrict the analysis to those men whose child's work activities were available for at least a nine-month period. This reduced the sample to 333 men with work activity information for their children. This number was further reduced to 293 since on some key variables no information was given by the father. Thus, the sample size for the micro-level regression analysis is 293. However, in cross tabulations larger samples are used whenever relevant. For example, if data on work input are not required, the tabulations are based on 1,095 married men. Further, many fathers had more than one child for which work activity information is available, resulting in data on 773 children which are used for the tabulations on child labour and child schooling.

Results and Discussions

This section is organized into two parts. The first provides an overview of children's work on the basis of time input for types of activities, and sex differentials for schoolgoing and non-schoolgoing children for selected social and demographic variables. This preliminary analysis provides the background for the regression analysis, presented in the second part of this section, on determinants of child labour and schooling, and their effects on parental fertility.

An Overview of Child Work

The data on the extent of child schooling and child labour separately for the high and low child labour districts are shown in Table 6.2. The percentage of boys and girls attending school in low child labour districts is slightly higher than the proportions in the high child labour districts. Among those not attending schools, the average time spent on directly productive work by both boys and girls from the high child labour districts, as expected, is higher than that spent by children from the low child labour districts. Even among those going to school, the extent of child labour in the high child labour districts is higher than in the low child labour districts. All these differences are in the expected directions except the time spent by schoolgoing girls in directly productive work.

Table 6.2 Average time input (in hours) per day of schoolgoing and non-schoolgoing children in different work activities by place of residence and sex of the child in rural Karnataka

Items	Boys			Girls		
	HCLD	LCLD	Combined	HCLD	LCLD	Combined
Number of children	203	141	344	217	167	384
Percentage attending school	64	69	66	42	51	46
	Average time input (hours) per day					
Schoolgoing						
Household work	0.76	0.72	0.74	1.68	1.35	1.52
Directly productive work	1.23	1.06	1.16	0.47	0.53	0.50
In school and related	3.22	3.92	3.52	3.16	3.76	3.45
Total	5.21	5.70	5.42	5.31	5.64	5.47
Non-schoolgoing						
Household work	1.13	1.96	1.41	3.12	3.52	3.28
Directly productive work	4.94	4.25	4.71	2.93	2.60	2.80
Total	6.07	6.21	6.12	6.05	6.12	6.08

HCLD: High child labour districts
LCLD: Low child labour districts

The time use of children aged 5–14 years in different work activities based on the data collected in the monthly survey is presented in Table 6.3. The findings demonstrate that children in the study area perform a variety of activities useful to their families from a very young age which is in conformity with the observations made earlier in several studies. Age and sex of the child seem to play an important role in shaping the activities in which they are engaged. Children put in an increasing amount of time on more productive activities as they grow older, and the average time spent working for wages is especially high among children in the 12–14 year age group. Girls in all age groups spend more time on activities related to food preparation than boys. Boys on the other hand spend more time in tending family livestock and working on the family farm. Sex differentials in market work are not large and time spent on 'trade' is insignificant for both boys and girls.

Table 6.3 Average time input in hours per child per day in different work activities

Sex	Age group	Activity: Household work: Related to food preparation*	Household work: Other**	Household work: Total	Directly productive work: Related to own live stock	Directly productive work: On own farm etc.	Directly productive work: On family trade	Directly productive work: For wages	Directly productive work: Total	All work	Schooling	Total
Boys	5–7	0.06	0.97	1.04	0.49	0.13	0.02	0.15	0.79	1.84	2.35	4.19
	8–9	0.06	0.90	0.96	1.36	0.57	0.07	0.15	2.17	3.13	2.43	5.57
	10–11	0.06	0.90	0.97	1.38	0.67	0.34	0.38	2.79	3.76	2.55	6.32
	12–14	0.09	0.90	1.00	1.84	0.89	0.09	1.57	4.40	5.40	1.74	7.14
	5–14	0.07	0.92	1.00	1.16	0.51	0.11	0.49	2.28	3.28	2.28	5.57
Girls	5–7	0.30	1.42	1.73	0.28	0.14	0.03	0.05	0.52	2.26	1.73	3.99
	8–9	0.49	1.58	2.08	0.96	0.36	0.04	0.24	1.62	3.70	1.90	5.61
	10–11	0.99	1.86	2.86	0.84	0.45	0.06	0.80	2.17	5.03	1.58	6.61
	12–14	1.63	1.99	3.63	0.84	0.74	0.09	1.60	3.27	6.90	0.83	7.74
	5–14	0.77	1.67	2.45	0.65	0.38	0.05	0.58	1.68	4.13	1.54	5.68

* Includes winnowing and cleaning of foodgrains and vegetables before cooking, cooking, serving food to family members, etc.
** Includes fetching water, washing clothes, sweeping house, washing floors, fuel collection, child care, running errands, etc.

The time input of children in school shows a particularly sharp decline in the 12–14 year age group, indicating a stronger demand for child time for other activities considered more useful for the family. The decline is sharper among girls aged 12–14 years, which may reflect the practice of withdrawing girls from school after they attain puberty. Data on time use obtained separately for schoolgoing and non-schoolgoing children support this (See Table 6.4). Moreover, school attendance is higher among boys than girls in all age groups.

Table 6.4 Average time input in hours per day of schoolgoing and non-schoolgoing children in different work activities by age and sex

	Percentage in school	Schoolgoing children			Non-schoolgoing children		No. of children
		HH work	DP work	Schooling	HH work	DP work	
Boys							
5–7	78	0.70	0.62	3.16	2.04	1.58	113
8–9	74	0.64	1.58	3.35	1.76	3.95	84
10–11	63	0.84	1.25	4.00	1.15	5.61	73
12–14	40	0.93	1.68	4.20	1.03	6.34	74
5–14	66	0.74	1.16	3.52	1.41	4.71	344
Girls							
5–7	59	1.16	0.36	3.08	2.60	0.85	137
8–9	56	1.57	0.52	3.46	2.71	3.01	75
10–11	39	1.95	0.74	4.04	3.43	3.06	89
12–14	23	2.18	0.57	3.94	3.97	4.08	83
5–14	46	1.52	0.50	3.45	3.27	2.81	384

Note: Out of the 773 children, 45 were going to school for only part of the year and are not included in the table. Therefore, Tables 6.5 and 6.6 are based on only 728 children.

HH work = Household work
DP work = Directly productive work

Differentials in work input among schoolgoing and non-schoolgoing children are large. Total time spent on all work (household and productive) by boys and girls not going to school increases from less than four hours at age 5–7 to more than seven hours at age 12–14; while the time spent on work for those attending school increases from about an hour and a half at ages 5–7 to about two and a half hours at ages 12–14.

School attendance of boys and girls and their work input by selected background variables are presented in Tables 6.5 and 6.6. Ownership of productive assets by the family seems to increase children's work except in families that own the largest amounts of land (10 acres plus) or the largest number of livestock (six plus). Hiring of labour from outside the household for certain types of activities was found to be characteristic of these families.

Table 6.5 Average time input (in hours) per day of schoolgoing and non-schoolgoing boys in different work activities by background variables

	BOYS						
Background variables	Schoolgoing				Not schoolgoing		N
	% attending school	Household work	Directly productive work	In school and related	Household work	Directly productive work	
1	2	3	4	5	6	7	8
Education of father (years of schooling completed)							
nil	51	0.69	1.41	2.93	1.36	4.64	131
1–4	65	0.73	1.27	3.55	1.37	5.18	110
5–9	80	0.91	0.93	4.05	1.80	3.63	75
10 and more	100	0.52	0.73	3.81	-	-	28
Size of the cultivated landholdings (in acres)							
nil	59	0.92	0.71	3.57	2.03	4.35	80
Less than 2	71	0.79	1.54	3.62	1.26	4.30	51
2–5	64	0.66	1.23	3.75	1.54	4.68	91
5–10	67	0.82	1.20	3.22	0.96	5.26	64
10 and more	72	0.53	1.19	3.38	0.66	5.05	58
No. of livestock at home							
nil	64	0.95	0.63	3.49	2.18	3.44	87
1–2	64	0.78	1.27	3.58	1.29	5.01	86
3–5	62	0.58	1.61	2.81	1.23	5.11	77
6 and more	71	0.65	1.17	4.00	0.84	5.36	94

Table 6.5 (cont.)

	BOYS						
Background variables	Schoolgoing				Not schoolgoing		N
	% attending school	Household work	Directly productive work	In school and related	Household work	Directly productive work	
1	2	3	4	5	6	7	8
Presence of younger children (0–4 years) in the family							
Yes	59	0.88	1.06	3.20	1.73	4.16	191
No	74	0.61	1.25	3.85	0.77	5.84	153
Presence of grandparents in the family							
Yes	78	0.65	1.20	3.40	1.67	4.43	86
No	62	0.78	1.14	3.56	1.39	4.74	258
Caste							
Lingayat	82	0.62	1.02	3.53	1.55	4.89	50
Vokkaliga	75	0.50	1.37	3.40	1.03	5.15	24
Scheduled castes	37	0.81	2.12	2.32	1.64	4.57	43
Scheduled tribes	50	0.79	1.87	2.54	1.41	5.49	26
Brahmins, Christians, Vys, Jains	95	0.60	0.57	3.97	*	*	21
Backward communities	55	0.82	1.10	3.56	1.42	5.15	14
Artisans	71	0.97	0.99	4.19	1.13	4.47	35
Muslims	91	0.69	1.10	3.47	0.80	4.38	32
Father's aspiration level							
Low	59	0.72	1.16	3.22	1.24	4.96	164
Moderate	68	0.72	1.13	3.70	1.76	4.25	138
High	83	0.87	1.22	3.91	0.94	4.92	42
Income per adult in the household (in rupees)							
Less than 800	57	0.91	1.40	3.40	1.58	4.56	81
800–1,499	62	0.80	1.14	3.38	1.29	4.46	95
1,500–2,999	62	0.69	1.08	3.45	1.40	5.17	108
3,000 & more	90	0.59	1.07	3.88	1.07	3.32	60

* Frequencies are too small

Table 6.6 Average time input (in hours) per day of schoolgoing and non-schoolgoing girls in different work activities by background variables

Background variables	GIRLS						
	Schoolgoing				Not school going		N
	% attending school	Household work	Directly productive work	In school and related	Household work	Directly productive work	
1	2	3	4	5	6	7	8
Education of father (years of schooling completed)							
nil	28	1.59	0.66	3.08	3.22	2.74	158
1–4	47	1.30	0.53	3.36	3.36	2.88	113
5–9	61	1.46	0.42	3.61	3.26	2.77	81
10 and more	97	1.90	0.31	3.92	*	*	32
Size of the landholdings (cultivated in acres)							
nil	43	1.44	0.34	3.32	3.43	2.44	105
Less than 2	48	1.83	0.59	2.98	2.72	2.81	50
2–5	51	1.52	0.57	3.77	3.60	3.05	105
5–10	37	1.49	0.58	3.99	3.24	2.87	62
10 and more	50	1.41	0.49	3.04	2.88	3.03	62
No. of livestock at home							
nil	42	1.59	0.33	3.15	3.60	2.14	97
1–2	45	1.50	0.61	3.47	3.27	3.41	99
3–5	41	1.63	0.43	3.39	3.15	2.83	88
6 and more	55	1.41	0.58	3.70	3.03	2.84	100
Presence of younger children (0–4 years) in the family							
Yes	40	1.86	0.48	3.17	3.49	2.53	217
No	54	1.21	0.51	3.71	2.89	3.26	167
Presence of grandparents in the family							
Yes	55	1.59	0.59	3.48	3.01	2.86	119
No	42	1.48	0.44	3.43	3.36	2.78	265
Caste							
Lingayat	63	1.67	0.46	3.62	3.33	3.00	67
Vokkaliga	47	1.47	0.81	3.90	2.68	4.56	30
Scheduled caste	16	0.97	0.55	2.92	2.89	2.61	62

Table 6.6 (cont.)

Background variables	GIRLS						
	Schoolgoing				Not schoolgoing		N
	% attending school	Household work	Directly productive work	In school and related	Household work	Directly productive work	
1	2	3	4	5	6	7	8
Caste (cont)							
Scheduled tribe	32	1.12	0.71	2.71	3.11	1.75	28
Brahmins, Christians, Vys, Jains	87	1.47	0.35	4.36	*	*	15
Backward communities	45	1.16	0.53	3.39	3.64	2.64	107
Artisans	48	1.62	0.59	3.75	3.31	3.02	42
Muslims	64	1.36	0.25	2.77	4.19	2.85	33
Father's aspiration level							
Low	34	1.71	0.68	3.08	3.11	2.99	171
Moderate	52	1.51	0.41	3.58	3.53	2.63	154
High	66	1.61	0.41	3.73	3.28	2.36	59
Income per adult in the household (in Rs)							
Less than 800	44	1.58	0.65	2.82	3.39	2.82	77
800–1,499	39	1.38	0.63	3.70	3.28	2.70	111
1,500–2,999	39	1.38	0.41	3.44	3.04	2.84	124
3,000 & above	72	1.73	0.38	3.65	3.98	2.99	72

* Frequencies are too small

The father's education seems to have an important bearing on the school attendance of children. All children go to school in cases where the father has a minimum of ten years of schooling, which suggests the desire of educated fathers to have educated children. Similarly, aspiration level of the father also has a significant positive relationship with child schooling. However, the presence of younger siblings in the household depresses school attendance, but the presence of grandparents increases schooling, suggesting work substitution among them. The findings for caste membership (a proxy for socioeconomic level), indicate that higher castes have higher school attendance of children while scheduled castes have the lowest school attendance of children.

The effects of child labour on child schooling and parental fertility can be assessed by comparing high and low child labour districts in terms of averages and percentages. This is done by considering all children in the household as well as by considering one child per household. Results, shown in Table 6.7, clearly indicate that demand for child labour decreases child schooling, and increases the demand for children and, perhaps, actual parental fertility by reducing the chances of contraceptive use. Whether or not the effect of child labour on parent fertility desires and contraceptive use are independent of the effect of child schooling is tested in the next section by using multiple regression analysis.

Table 6.7 Indexes of fertility, contraceptive use, child labour, and schooling by high and low child labour districts in rural Karnataka

Indexes	For all children in households			One child per household		
	HCLD	LCLD	Combined	HCLD	LCLD	Combined
1. Mean hours per day per child	3.91	3.44	3.74	4.01	3.19	3.71
2. Percentage in school	48	61	53	48	59	52
3. Time in school	-	-	-	1.22	1.95	1.49
4. Average ideal family size	3.04	2.95	3.01	3.04	2.95	3.01
5. Percentage use of contraception	41	61	48	41	61	48

HCLD: High child labour districts
LCLD: Low child labour districts

Results of Regression Analysis

Two types of analysis are conducted to study determinants of child labour and schooling and their effects on fertility. The first analysis is based on all children between 5 and 14 years of age. Child schooling in this analysis is measured by the percentage of all children aged 5–14 years of the respondent who are attending school. Child labour is measured by the mean hours per day per child in all work activities for children aged 5–14 years. For schoolgoing children, the mean work on school days and holidays is computed separately and weighted by the average number of school days and holidays to obtain the overall mean. Since these indexes for each father are usually based on a small number of children in the 5–14 years age group (the denominator was one in 67 cases, 2 in 85 caes, 3 in 88, 4 in 39, 5 in 12, 6 in one, and 7 in one case), their values may be subject to large random errors. The effect of this source of error is minimized in the second analysis which is based on only one child per family selected randomly on the computer. The results of the first analysis are briefly discussed as a background.

Results for All Children

This analysis focuses on the work input and schooling of all children aged 5–14 of the interviewed father. The simultaneous equations for child labour and child schooling showed that in addition to the inverse reciprocal relationship, adult female work input has a positive effect and rainfall has a negative effect on work input of children. The equation for child schooling shows a positive effect of aspiration level and education of the father, and a negative effect of membership in a scheduled caste. A number of other background variables included in the analysis did not show any significant effect on either child schooling or child labour.

As expected, the ideal family size increases with child labour and decreases with child schooling. The use of contraception decreases with child labour and increases with child schooling. The effect of child schooling is independent of child labour and the effect of child labour is independent of child schooling. However, after controlling for the background factors, neither child labour nor child schooling show a significant relationship with ideal family size and contraceptive practice. The lack of an independent effect of child schooling and child labour inputs on contraception and fertility desires is contrary to expectations based on earlier studies. Whether or not these results are artifacts of the large random errors in the indexes of child labour and child schooling is tested by restricting the analysis to only one child per family.

Results for One Child per Family

In this analysis, an individual child, selected at random from the children in the 5–14 age group, is used as the unit of analysis, along with the information on the father. Child schooling is split into two variables, whether or not a child goes to school, and time in hours per day spent in school. In the first portion of the analysis the dichotomous child schoolgoing variable is used as an antecedent variable for child work input, which in turn is used as an antecedent variable for time spent by children in school. Conceptually, whether or not a child goes to school is affected by such background characteristics as father's education and his aspiration level; schoolgoing status of a child then affects his/her work input; and both together affect the time spent by the child in school. Thus, even for schoolgoing children, the time spent in school will depend on the demand or need for his/her work input. An advantage of this model is that the individual child's age in years and sex can be used as controls for all three endogenous variables: schoolgoing, work input, and time in school. In the second portion of the analysis work input and schooling are utilized as antecedent variables for ideal family size and contraceptive practice.

Results of multiple regression analysis of schoolgoing status, child labour and time spent in school are shown in Table 6.8. Whether or not a child goes to school is determined by his/her age and sex, father's education and aspiration level and the caste to which the family belongs. Schooling is inversely related to age, and is lower among females than males. Father's education and aspiration level as hypothesized exert a significant positive effect on schooling while scheduled caste membership affects schooling negatively.

Whether or not a child goes to school affects both the extent of child labour and time spent in school. The extent of child labour and the time spent in school are also correlated. This association between the two variables is not spurious and is not caused by a common third factor—whether or not a child goes to school. The correlation coefficient between child labour and time in school, -0.634, reduces to -0.172 after partialling out the effect of the child's schoolgoing status, and remains significant statistically.

Table 6.8 Standardized regression coefficients for child labour and schooling regressed on selected variables

Independent variables	schoolgoing status of child		child labour		time in school	
	r	ß	*r*	ß	*r*	ß
Schoolgoing status	—		-0.658	-0.517	0.865	0.656
Child labour	-0.658		—	—	-0.634	-0.263
Female work input	-0.170		0.174	0.105	0.129	—
Rainfall	0.093		-0.190	-0.142	0.171	—
Landholding	0.074		-0.043	ns	0.011	-0.096
SC membership	-0.341	-0.244	0.175	ns	-0.380	-0.068
Aspiration level	0.260	0.172	-0.233	-0.086	0.283	ns
Education of father	0.401	0.239	-0.315	—	0.457	0.121
Presence of younger children	-0.108		0.117	0.151	-0.141	—
Age of child	-0.144	-0.150	0.530	0.494	-0.041	0.201
Sex of child	0.220	0.192	-0.110	ns	0.214	ns
R^2		0.288		0.684		0.806

Note: 1) *r* = Zero order correlation coefficients

ß =Standardized regression coefficients when all significant paths are included

— : not included in the equation

ns : not significant at 5% level

2) Cattle, dominant caste membership, family type, opportunity consciousness, school accessibility were not significant in the equations and hence are not shown in the table.

Child labour, in addition to the schoolgoing status of the child, is also affected significantly by age, i.e. older children tend to work more, and by the presence of younger siblings who no doubt increase work through the additional demands of child care. Female work input, aspiration level and rainfall also exert significant effects on child labour; the effect of the first factor is positive while the effects of the latter two are negative. Education of the father is hypothesized to have an indirect effect on child labour through schoolgoing status. Inclusion of the father's education among the explanatory variables in the equation for child labour does not change the effect of other variables on child labour. Moreover, the beta coefficient reflecting the effect of the father's education on child labour does not remain significant statistically (results not shown in the table).

The average time spent in school by a child is affected positively by whether or not s/he goes to school and negatively by the extent of child labour. In addition, it is affected positively by age of child and education of father and negatively by landholding and scheduled caste membership. These effects are the *direct* effects of these variables net of the effects of schooling and child labour and are significant statistically. In addition, *indirect* effects, which are also significant, upon time in school are transmitted through schooling or child labour, by background factors: father's education, aspiration level and scheduled caste membership through schooling; and rainfall, female work input and presence of younger siblings through child labour.

The results of the regression analysis of ideal family size and family planning practice on child labour, time in school and other selected variables are presented in Table 6.9.

When ideal family size and contraceptive practices are regressed on child labour and time in school, the independent effects of both factors remain significant statistically. Ideal family size increases with the extent of child labour and decreases with the time spent in school. The practice of contraception increases with both the extent of child labour and time in school. The beta coefficients, measuring the direct effects of child labour on ideal family size as well as contraceptive practices, however, do not remain significant statistically after controlling for the effects of background factors. In comparison, time in school continues to exhibit significant negative and positive effects, respectively, on ideal family size and contraceptive practice. Although child labour is not significantly related to either of these variables, it does affect them indirectly through its negative effect on time in school. The resultant effect on ideal family size is positive while the effect on contraceptive practice is negative. Therefore, child labour would be expected to exert a pronatalistic effect on fertility indirectly through its inverse relationship with schooling, which exhibited an antinatalistic effect on fertility. Replacement of time spent in school by the schoolgoing status variable in regression analysis of ideal family size and contraceptive practice does not affect the results of the analysis. Children's schooling reduces ideal family size and increases the use of contraceptives independent of the effects of other variables included in the analysis.

Table 6.9 Standardized regression coefficients for ideal family size and contraceptive practice regressed on child labour and schooling and selected variables

Independent variables	Ideal family size			Contraceptive practice		
	r	*ß*	*ß'*	*r*	*ß*	*ß'*
Child labour	0.130	0.015	-0.050(ns)	-0.118	+0.077	0.057(ns)
Time in school	-0.191	-0.182	-0.199	0.259	0.308	0.264
Female work input	0.055	—	ns	-0.160	—	-0.118
Opportunity consciousness	-0.142	—	-0.157	0.212	—	0.167
Number of living children	0.241	—	0.266	0.166	—	0.127
R^2			0.118			0.137

Note: 1) *r* = Zero order correlation coefficients
ß = Standardized regression coefficients with only child labour and time in school in the equation
ß' = Standardized regression coefficients when all significant paths are ncluded
— : not included in the equation
ns : not significant at 5% level
2) Landholding, caste membership, family type, aspiration level, education of father, past mortality experience, sex composition of children and age of youngest child were not significant in both the equations and hence are not shown in the table.

Summary and Conclusions

This study had three objectives. The first was to examine the nature and extent of work engaged in by children in rural Karnataka. The results indicated that on average children spend four hours a day on work, whether household work or directly productive work, and that their participation increases with age as expected. Sex differentials were found both in the nature of work, greater household work by girls and greater directly productive work by boys, and in the time spent on work. That is, girls put in longer hours than boys because relatively fewer girls than boys go to school.

The second objective was to examine the relationship between child labour and schooling and their determinants. A significant negative reciprocal relationship between these factors was found. The most important predictors of child labour were age and the presence of younger children, which both showed positive effects. Age and sex of child, father's education, his aspiration and membership in scheduled caste were the predictors of whether or not a child goes to school. However, age of child and father's education were the primary predictors of time in school, and their effects were also positive. Contrary to the popular belief that children from poor families work more, income and other socioeconomic factors did not significantly affect children's work input.

The third and final objective was to analyse the effect of child labour and schooling on parental fertility. Although no direct relationship was found between child labour and fertility, child labour did significantly affect fertility indirectly by reducing the time spent in school. Since schooling has an antinatalistic effect on fertility, the overall effect of child labour on fertility is positive. This relationship persisted net of the significant negative effects on fertility of father's opportunity consciousness and number of living children. Further, socioeconomic factors such as landholding and father's education proved insignificant in the relationship. Hence, it would appear that both reductions in the incidence of child labour and increases in the proportions of children going to school and remaining in school will contribute to a reduction in fertility.

Policy Implications

Child labour was found to exert a significant positive effect on fertility through its effect on schooling, and the latter factor was found to exert a significant negative effect on fertility. Hence, policies directed at reducing the requirements for child labour and increasing the chances of children remaining in school would be expected to contribute to a reduction in fertility. Though primary

education is compulsory and is practically free, school enrolment rates are low and the drop-out rates, especially among females, are high. One major factor contributing to these rates is that children are retained at home for work. For example, we have found that non-schoolgoing children put in an average of four hours of work input more per day than schoolgoing children. A policy which would compensate families for this work may prove to be very expensive; however, a more practical alternative would be to eliminate the need for some of the work done by children. A large portion of the work of children consists of tending cattle and doing routine household chores such as fetching water from a well or river, grinding spices, cleaning and washing foodgrains and vegetables for cooking, and fetching firewood. A policy which would provide better water and fuel facilities for villages, clean and ready-to-cook foodgrains, and arrangements for communal tending of cattle would make a contribution to a reduction in the need for children's labour and allow them time to attend school. This would ultimately contribute to a reduction in fertility through the resulting higher rates of contraception among parents.

Policies directed to reduce the need for children's labour would allow them to go to school and spend more time in school-related activities in areas where schooling facilities are easily accessible. In other areas, making schooling facilities more accessible would increase the proportion of children, especially girls, who go to school. This, in turn, would contribute to a reduction in child labour, to an increase in time spent in school, and to lower fertility.

References

Cain, Mead T., 1977. 'The Economic Activities of Children in a Village in Bangladesh.' *Population and Development Review*, **3** (3), pp.201–27.

Caldwell, J. C., Jalaluddin, A. K. M., Caldwell, P. & Cosford, W., 1979. 'The Control of Activity in Bangladesh.' Australian National University, Canberra, mimeo.

Da Vanzo, J., 1972. 'The Determinants of Family Formation in Chile 1960: An Econometric Study of Female Labour Force Participation, Marriage and Fertility Decisions.' R-830-AID, Santa Monica, Rand Corporation.

De Tray, D., 1983. 'Child Labour in Malaysia.' *Population and Development Review*, **9** (3), pp.437–55.

Duncan, O. D., 1975. *Introduction to Structural Models*, New York, Academic Press.

Harman, A. J., 1970. 'Fertility and Economic Behaviour of Families in the Philippines.' RM-6385-AID, Santa Monica, Rand Corporation.

Kasarada, J. D., 1971. 'Economic Structure and Fertility: A Comparative Analysis.' *Demography*, **8** (3), pp.307–17.

Mamdani, Mahmood, 1972. *The Myth of Population Control: Family, Caste and Class in an Indian Village*. New York, Monthly Review Press.

Maurer, K., Ralajazak, M. & Schultz, R. P., 1973. 'Marriage, Fertility and Labour Force Participation of Thai Women: An Econometric Study.' R-829-AID/RF, Santa Monica, Rand Corporation.

Nadkarni, M. V., 1976. 'Over Population and the Rural Poor.' *Economic and Political Weekly*, (Bombay) **11** (31–33), pp.1163–72.

Nag, Moni, White, B. N. F., & Peet, C. R., 1978. 'An Anthropological Approach to the Study of Economic Value of Children in Java and Nepal.' *Current Anthropology*, **19** (2), pp.293–306.

Reddy, A. K. N., 1980. 'Rural Energy Consumption Patterns: A Field Study.' ASTRA, Indian Institute of Science, Bangalore, mimeo.

Rosenzweig, M. R. & Evension, Robert, 1977. 'Fertility, Schooling and the Economic Contributions of Children in Rural India: An Econometric Analysis.' *Econometrica*, **45** (5), pp.1065–79.

Rosenzweig, M. R., 1978. 'The Value of Children's Time, Family Size and Non-Household Child Activities in a Developing Country: Evidence from Household Data,' *Research in Population Economics*, J. L. Simon (ed.). Greenwich, Jain Press Inc.

Schultz, T. Paul, 1970. 'Fertility Patterns and their Determinants in the Arab Middle East.' RM 5978, FF, Rand Corporation.

Vlassoff, M., 1979. 'Labour Demand Economic Utility of Children: A Case Study in Rural India.' *Population Studies*, **33** (3), pp.415–28.

7 Methodological Issues in Assessing the Fertility Impact of Development Projects

Anrudh K. Jain and John Stoeckel

Introduction

Formulation of development policies, and their implementation through programs and projects, are primarily concerned with the issues related to the social and economic development of a country. These activities rarely consider their second order effects on the demographic parameters. Special population policies are designed and implemented usually through family planning programs to address the issues of rapid population growth in developing countries. The 1974 World Population Conference brought into sharp focus the relative importance and contributions of the nationally sponsored and organized family planning programs against socioeconomic development in the decrease of population growth rates. Inclusion of development programs in the search for interventions that might reduce fertility, sometimes called the 'Bucharest prescription,' however, was not uniformly accepted. Berelson, for example, in 1978 noted that 'the objective of the whole exercise is to expedite that [fertility] reduction in order to hasten development; so recommending the latter as a way to achieve the former rather misses the point' (p. 607).

Population professionals, concerned with a potential decrease in funding for population related activities, pointed out that the reallocation of population funds to development programs in general is unlikely to hasten the reduction of population growth. Such arguments were based on the fact that a small fraction of development budgets—less than 3 percent—was allocated to family planning programs and related biomedical and social science research. Adding these funds to general developmental activities would not have substantially increased the total funds available for development. Moreover, very little was known about the antinatalistic effects of specific development programs to make it possible for either to add population funds to a specific development program or to consider reallocation of total development funds. What was missing was the empirical information about the effect of specific development projects on demographic parameters—especially fertility.

In this book we have presented results from five studies designed to assess the impact of development on fertility. The fertility impacts of rural electrification, guaranteed price support, land settlement, and their combinations in Sri Lanka are presented in Chapter 2. Chapters 3 and 4 focus upon the impacts on fertility of rural electrification and irrigation projects, respectively, in Northeast Thailand. Chapter 5 deals with the effects of female employment and occupational settings on fertility in the Philippines, and Chapter 6 analyzes the effects upon fertility of child labor and schooling in rural Karnataka, India.

This chapter deals with an overview of methodological issues involved in assessing the impact of development projects on fertility. The general issues of control and selectivity, model specification, and level of analysis are discussed in the light of the experience gained from the five empirical studies. Finally, implications for future research in this area are discussed.

Methodological Issues

Development related public interventions are designed and implemented at aggregate levels, usually defined by territorial boundaries. Fertility behavior, on the other hand, refers to the behavior of individual couples. The rationale for expecting the effect of macro-level factors on the micro-level behavior flows from the assumption that 'social context or social normative variables must affect fertility' (Freedman, 1985, p. 269). Inputs provided through development projects influence the social context within which decisions about family size are made by individual couples. Specification and measurement of these linkages are essential ingredients in assessing the impact of a development project on fertility. Whether and how to link the macro-level interventions with the micro-level behavior, thus, are some of the major issues in research related to the measurement of the impact of development projects on fertility.

These issues in a broader context have been addressed by other investigators involved in the collection and analysis of data on community-level variables through the WFS program (Casterline, 1985a, 1985b). Since this program was not specifically designed to study the impact of development projects on fertility, it paid very little attention to the specification and measurement of the linkages between development project outputs and fertility. Instead these analyses mainly focused on documenting whether or not community-level variables have any effect on individual-level fertility that is independent of household and individual-level socioeconomic characteristics.

The major departure of the studies included in this book consists of the fact that, first, they were specifically designed to measure the effect of development project outputs on fertility and, second, they specified and measured the linkages between these outputs and fertility. The specification of these linkages was based on the assumption that development project outputs affect social and economic characteristics of couples which in turn influences demand for children. These changes in the demand structure are translated into actual fertility through important proximate determinants. Consideration of this causal chain of events brings into focus the magnitude of the effect one should expect and the time frame during which such effects are actually realized. Consideration of methodological issues involved in the measurement of all the variables included in this chain linking development outputs to fertility and consideration of appropriate time lags involved at each step further lowers one's expectations. Judged against these expectations, the results of the studies included in this book are quite encouraging and positive. These studies do show that the total effects of various development projects on fertility are significant and in expected directions. The indirect effects of project outputs, i.e. the effects transmitted through individual social and economic characteristics and proximate determinants on fertility are also significant. The disappointment comes from the fact that we are left with large effects of development projects on fertility which are not accounted for by the links specified by the models used in these studies. This implies that the models used were not completely specified. These residual effects were not included in individual chapters but are discussed later on in this chapter. Considering the magnitude of these residuals, one might be tempted to conclude that development projects have considerable and significant 'independent' effects on fertility. But such a conclusion will not be accurate.

As described in Chapter 1, all studies included in this book utilized a cross-sectional approach which relies on information collected at one point in time. The study design was based on stratification of villages or individuals. Outputs of development projects were used as the stratification variables. Outputs in the Sri Lanka and Thailand studies were measured in terms of the presence of governmental sponsored infrastructural facilities. In the Philippine and the Indian studies, outputs referred to the outcome of development process—occupational setting in the Philippine study and child labour in the Indian study. The effects of development project outputs were estimated by comparing individuals from strata with and without the relevant project outputs. Appropriate statistical controls were used to minimize the effect of selectivity bias which is inherent in assessing the impact of development on fertility through this type of design.

Research on fertility impacts of development, as in other areas of social science, requires models or explanatory frameworks which can adequately describe the nature and direction of relationships between variables. The complexity of the interrelationships between fertility and development makes this a formidable task particularly since developmental outputs must operate indirectly through a host of factors to affect fertility. Four issues usually encountered in attempting to specify and disentangle variables and their relationships are simultaneity, multicollinearity, time lags and incompleteness. The selectivity bias and these four issues are discussed below.

Control and Selectivity

The nature of research in the area of fertility impact studies makes it extremely difficult to control for all relevant factors contributing to socioeconomic change and affecting fertility behavior. For example, a variety of development programs might be simultaneously implemented in the same geographic area and thus attribution of fertility change to specific program outputs would require natural or statistical controls. Seldom are there field situations which lend themselves to natural experiments where a control area without the outputs of interest can be identified. Hence, an approach which attempts a semblance of control and takes into account the multitude of factors and their changes poses a formidable problem for researchers studying fertility impacts of development.

A related problem in assessing the fertility impacts of development projects is how to minimize the effect of the selectivity bias, which refers to a village or a household being 'self-selected' for exposure to development inputs on the basis of characteristics or attributes they already have. For example, geographic areas are selected to receive inputs based upon such specific criteria as suitability of administrative infrastructure, level of economic activity, and existing availability of services. These factors in turn will affect the impact the inputs will have upon the population and must necessarily be taken into account. At the household level, wealthier segments of a rural population are in a better position to afford the cost of new electricity lines under a rural electrification project and may be disproportionately represented among the recipients of the project. Therefore, it is important to attempt to control for relevant background factors of a population which affect both access to and receipt of development outputs.

The problems of control and selectivity have been attended to in the studies included in this book at the design stage utilizing stratification and at the analysis stage using statistical controls. In the studies on the fertility effects of multiple development projects in Sri Lanka and the effects of electrification and irrigation in Thailand, villages were stratified initially on the presence and absence of projects. Samples of villages were then selected from these respective strata. The study in India on child labor and schooling selected village samples from districts stratified on the basis of high and low incidences of child labor in separate regions; and in the Philippine study on the effects of female employment on fertility, areas were stratified on the basis of industrial setting before selecting the samples of individuals.

All the impact studies utilized statistical controls for additional exogenous variables that might contribute to selectivity and/or affect the outcome of their analyses. For example, in assessing the effects of mixes of development projects on occupation and income in the Sri Lanka study and the effects of irrigation and electrification on these variables in the Thai studies, educational attainment is included in the regression equation to control for its effect on occupation and income. Similarly, the effects of additional development outputs such as electrification in the Thai irrigation study and irrigation in the Thai electrification study are included in regression equations to control for their effects upon socioeconomic factors. The duration of marriage has been used as an additional control to minimize the effect of the life cycle variable on occupation, income, and fertility related variables.

Simultaneity. Relationships between variables may be simultaneous; for example, child labor-force participation and fertility. Among families at lower income levels, high fertility probably contributes to low school attendance rates and high child labor-force participation rates because of income constraints. However, at the same time, the availability of ample employment opportunities for children and the lack of educational opportunities may contribute to the higher fertility level of the families. Therefore, causal inferences from one variable to another become extremely tenuous.

The problem of simultaneity was encountered in the India study where child schooling and labor were considered as reciprocally related. To overcome this problem a recursive path model of analysis was utilized in which child schooling was split into two variables: whether or not a child goes to school, and time in hours per day spent in school. The dichotomous child school-going variable is then analyzed as an antecedent variable for child work input, which in turn is used as an antecedent variable for time in school.

Multicollinearity. There may be multicollinearity among the exogenous variables, that is, the variables may be highly intercorrelated so that it is difficult to determine their individual effects. Indicators of developmental output, for example increases in per capita income, educational enrolment, and labor-force participation rates, are generally highly intercorrelated and tend to change in similar directions over time. Finding enough divergent motion among these variables is difficult and creates a problem for separating out changes in fertility which can be attributed to them.

Multicollinearity in the impact studies was assessed by the usual means. That is, in addition to inspection of the simple correlations between independent variables, each independent variable was regressed on all other independent variables. In instances where the R^2 was 'high' the 'offending' variable was discarded. For example, in the Thai electrification study several village level measures of electrification initially included in the analysis were found to be highly intercorrelated. Hence, only one village level measure was utilized.

Time Lags. The time lags allowed for interactions between variables may be insufficient. Changes in fertility are seldom a short-term phenomenon; neither are the changes in socioeconomic and intermediate factors which must take place before the effects of development upon fertility become apparent.

The case of Taiwan provides an illustration of the effect that a time lag in the change in the socioeconomic structure of a population can have on fertility decline. Freedman *et al.* (1977) have shown that 23 percent of the decline in the crude birth rate in Taiwan during 1966–74 was attributable to education. Calculations presented in Table 7.1 also show that about 25 percent of the decline in the total fertility rate during 1966–74 can be attributed to changes in the education distribution of women in the childbearing period, 15–44 years of age. The remaining 75 percent of the decline in overall fertility was due to changes in education-specific fertility rates. Thus, three-fourths of the observed decline in fertility is attributable to changes in individual behavior, whereas one-fourth is attributable to changes in educational structure during 1966–74. These changes in the educational distribution of women 15–44 years of age are the outcome of changes that took place over a period of about forty years.

Table 7.1 Estimated total fertility rate per 1,000 women in Taiwan and decomposition of change during 1966–74

	Education-specific fertility	Education distribution	Estimated total fertility
1.	1966	1966	4663
2.	1966	1974	4286
3.	1974	1974	3152

		Absolute	Percent
4.	Change in total fertility during 1966–74:	*Absolute*	*Percent*
	a. Total: 1–3	1,511	100
	b. Due to change in education distribution:1–2	377	25
	c. Due to change in education specific fertility: 2–3	1,134	75

Estimates of the amount of time required for the education distribution to change are shown in Table 7.2. The distributions presented in columns (3) to (6) illustrate the changes in the education composition of women who entered the childbearing period around 1936, 1944, 1966 and 1974. Those women who entered their childbearing process in 1936 completed it around 1966, and those who entered their childbearing process around 1944 completed it around 1974. Slightly over 60 percent of women who entered their childbearing period in 1936 were illiterate in comparison to less than 3 percent who entered childbearing in 1974. Similarly, the proportions with at least a junior high school education increased from 7 percent in 1936 to about 47 percent in 1974. Thus it took about forty years for major changes in the educational structure to occur in Taiwan.

Table 7.2 Estimated Distribution of women 15–19 years by education attainment 1936–74, and education-specific total fertility rate in Taiwan, 1966 and 1974

	Total fertility rate		Estimated distribution of women 15–19 years			
Education	1966 (1)	1974 (2)	1936 (3)	1944 (4)	1966 (5)	1974 (6)
Illiterate	5,445	3,740	62.0	45.9	8.2	2.3
Literate	5,105	3,280	11.7	13.5	11.4	5.5
Primary	4,595	3,445	18.9	30.1	62.7	45.0
Junior high	3,025	2,440	3.0	5.1	14.5	39.0
Senior high	2,605	2,220	4.4	5.4	3.2	8.2
Total	4,675	2,935	100.0	100.0	100.0	100.0

This example illustrates that the changes in the socioeconomic structure and its effect on fertility could be expected to take a substantial period of time. Therefore, an analytical approach focussing upon short-term variations in fertility may miss the actual shifts in the development and socioeconomic variables and subsequent changes in fertility. This problem is minimized as much as possible in most of the studies included in this book by focussing upon measures of recent fertility (births in the past five years) and development projects initiated at substantially earlier periods in time. For example, in the Sri Lanka study the development projects were all implemented at least ten years prior to the initiation of the study. In the Philippine study, the employment-occupational status of women was measured prior to the beginning of the open birth interval—another indicator of recent fertility. A focus on recent fertility, however, introduced a large random noise due to the stochastic nature of the event—birth—and reduced the explanatory power of the model.

Incompleteness. Specification of relationships may be incomplete because key explanatory variables are omitted or not controlled for. For example, increasing women's labor-force participation through selected developmental outputs is expected to lead to lower fertility. However, it is becoming increasingly evident that it is not the participation *per se* but the type of participation and associated wage rates that contribute to lowering fertility. Studies which do not control for these factors and rely upon simple associations between women's participation and fertility can produce spurious inferences about the relationship.

This issue was illustrated in the Sri Lanka study. The participation of females in non-household occupations showed a positive relationship with contraceptive practice for the rural electrification project alone and two mixes of projects which included rural electrification with the guaranteed price scheme and with the land settlement scheme. However, for the three remaining projects, land settlement, guaranteed price scheme, and the combination of the two, the relationship between the participation of females in non-household occupations and contraceptive use was not significant. This suggested that it was not simply employment of females outside the household that will increase family planning practice but the type of employment. Additional analysis of the distribution of the types of occupations between the rural electrification projects and the other projects provided support for this assertion. That is, in contrast to the other projects, the rural electrification projects are characterized by high participation of females in 'public sector' occupations, and it is among these occupations that contraceptive use is the highest.

The issue of incompleteness is integrally related to the model specification and can affect the results and their interpretation. This effect is further elaborated in the next section.

Model Specification

This section deals with the issues related to model specification and level of analysis, both of which affect the measurement of and inferences about the fertility impact of development projects. We do not intend to review the literature on impact studies in general. Instead we will focus on issues faced by us in measuring the impact of development projects on fertility through cross-sectional surveys.

The general model used in studies included in this book assumes that the effect of development on fertility is indirect, i.e. it operates through changes in individual and household-level socioeconomic characteristics which are directly affected by development project outputs. These characteristics are assumed to affect the demand for children, which is translated into the effect on actual fertility through changes in proximate factors. This model and the book do not include population projects, which can directly influence attitudes toward family size or such proximate determinants as the use of contraception.

The impact of development project outputs on fertility can be measured by using the community-level, individual-level, and multi-level analyses. In the community-level analysis, the interest is in explaining fertility differences among communities and for this purpose outputs of a development project at the community level are related to the aggregate fertility. In the individual-level and multi-level analyses, the interest is in the explanation of fertility differences among individuals. In the individual-level analysis, outputs of a development project at the individual level are related to the individual fertility behavior. In the multi-level analysis, outputs at community and individual levels are related to the individual-level fertility behavior. We have used the multi-level analysis in all the five studies presented in this book. After discussing the issues of measurement related to this approach, we will return to the community-level analysis which was used in these studies, but the results are not presented in the individual chapters for reasons discussed later on.

Let us consider rural electrification projects as an illustration to identify measurement issues. Let the output of rural electrification at the village level be denoted by X_6 and the individual-level fertility be denoted by X_0. The observed correlation coefficient, r_{06}, between the two, measures the total effect of rural electrification on fertility.

This total effect is made up of four components:

1. spurious effect due to selectivity biases, i.e. the village and households benefiting from electrification may be self selected;
2. indirect effect explained by the model;
3. indirect effect not explained by the model; and
4. residual random term.

If the model is completely specified, item 3 will be virtually zero. On the other hand, item 2 will be close to zero, if the model is not appropriately specified or if the project outputs have no effect on those factors which affect fertility. Lack of specification can be due to the exclusion of some proximate determinants of fertility or due to exclusion of some of those important background factors which are directly affected by the outputs of a development project, on the one hand, and in turn influence decisions about family size and adoption of fertility regulation methods. Similarly, the residual term can be further subdivided corresponding to the residual due to errors involved in the measurement of fertility, proximate determinants, and indirect determinants included in the model.

In the Sri Lanka study, the authors used education (X_4) and duration of marriage (X_5) to control for the effect of selectivity bias. They also used occupation (X_3) and income (X_2) to measure the direct effect of development project outputs on economic conditions at the household level, and the use of contraception (X_1) as one of the proximate determinants of fertility. The following set of equations describes the model:

$$X_o = p_{o1} X_1 + p_{o5} X_5 + p_{os} X_{os}$$

$$X_1 = p_{12} X_2 + p_{13} X_3 + p_{14} X_4 + p_{15} X_5 + p_{lt} X_t$$

$$X_2 = p_{23} X_3 + p_{24} X_4 + p_{25} X_5 + p_{26} X_6 + p_{2v} X_v$$

$$X_3 = p_{34} X_4 + p_{35} X_5 + p_{36} X_6 + p_{3u} X_u$$

where, the p_{ij} are the path coefficients representing the direct effect on variable i from variable j.

The total effect of development project (X_6) on fertility (X_o), r_{o6}, and use of contraception (X_1), r_{16}, can be decomposed by using the following two equations:

$$r_{o6} = p_{o1} r_{16} + p_{o5} X_{56} + p_{os} r_{6s} \quad (1)$$

$$r_{16} = p_{12} r_{26} + p_{13} r_{36} + P_{14} r_{46} + p_{15} r_{56} + p_{1t} r_{t6} \quad (2)$$

By substituting the value of r_{16} in the equation for r_{o6} and rearranging terms, we can decompose the total effect of rural electrification on fertility:

$$r_{o6} = p_{o1} (p_{12} r_{26} + p_{13} r_{36}) + [p_{o1} (p_{14} r_{46} + p_{15} r_{56})] + p_{o5} r_{56} + p_{o1} p_{1t} r_{t6} + p_{os} r_{6s} \quad (3)$$

Different terms in equation (3) are shown below:

1.	Total effect	r_{o6}
2.	Indirect effect explained by the model through occupation, income, and family planning.	$p_{o1} (p_{12} r_{26} + p_{13} r_{36})$
3.	Spurious effect due to associations with education and marital duration	$p_{o1} (p_{14} r_{46} + p_{15} r_{56}) + p_{o5} r_{56}$
4.	Residual associated with the measurement of family planning and lack of specification of indirect determinants.	$p_{o1} p_{1t} r_{t6}$
5.	Residual associated with the measurement of fertility and lack of specification of proximate determinants.	$p_{os} r_{6s}$

Based on the analysis carried out by authors of the Sri Lanka study, the complete models showing path coefficients for decomposing the effect of development project outputs on fertility through female characteristics are shown in Figures 7.1 and 7.2. From this analysis, we cannot separate that effect of project output on fertility which is due to lack of model specification from that effect which is due to random noise in the measurement of family

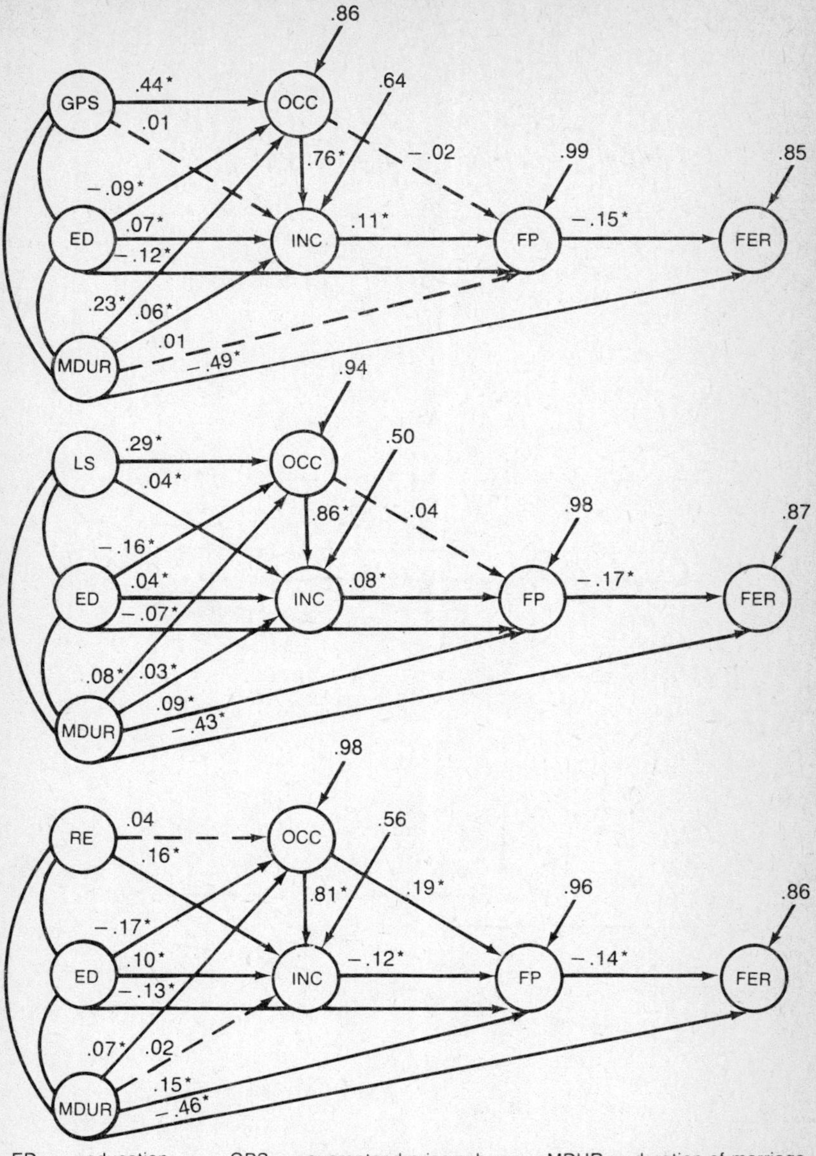

ED = education GPS = guaranteed price scheme MDUR = duration of marriage
FER = fertility INC = income OCC = occupation
FP = family planning LS = land settlement RE = rural electrification

Note: A broken line indicates that the effect is not significant. *Significant at the .001 level.

Figure 7.1 Path analysis of relationship between *individual* development programs, *female* socioeconomic status, family planning, and recent fertility

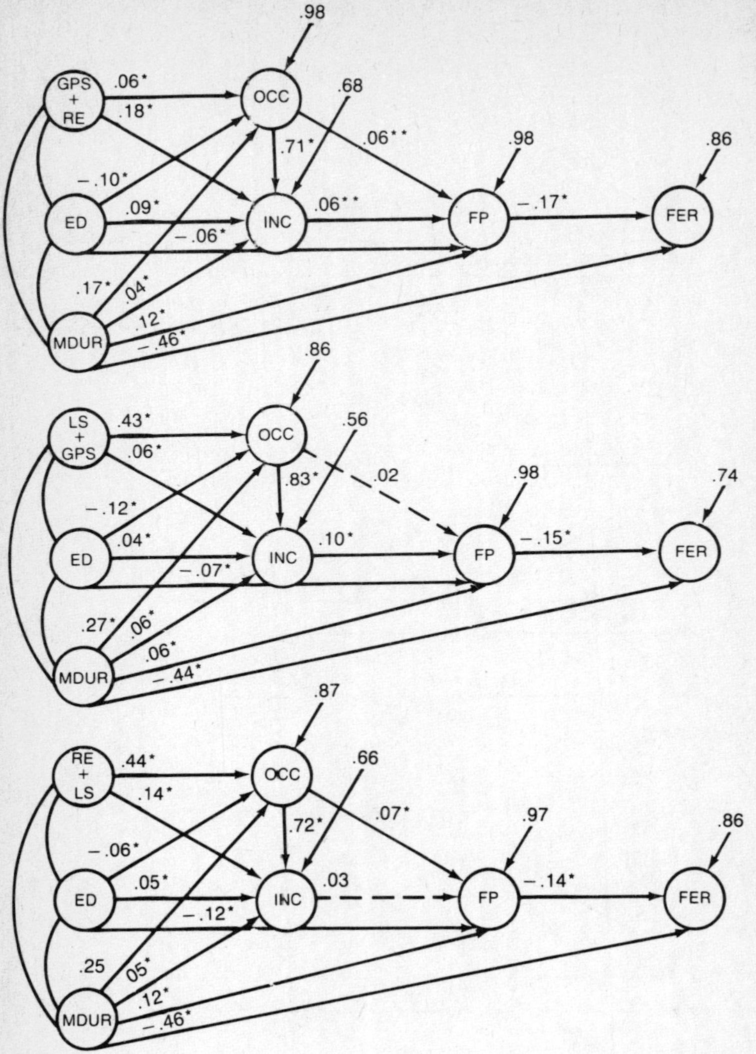

Key:

ED = education
FER = fertility (births in the last five years)
FP = family planning
GPS = guaranteed price scheme
INC = income
LS = land settlement
MDUR = duration of marriage
OCC = occupation
RE = rural electrification

Note: A broken line indicates that the effect is not significant.
*Significant at the .001 level. **Significant at the .01 level.

Figure 7.2 Path diagrams of relationship between *combination* of development programs, *female* socioeconomic status, family planning, and recent fertility planning and fertility indicators. Additional analysis is required to isolate these effects. The values of $p_{lt}\ r_{t6}$ can be estimated from equation (2) expressing r_{16} and the value of $p_{os}\ r_{6s}$ can be estimated from equation (1) on r_{06}. The magnitude of the indirect effect in item 2 above will be slightly different from those shown in Chapter 3 because a part of the correlations of project output with occupation and income (r_{26} and r_{36}) might be due to selectivity bias, i.e., due to the association of project output with education and duration of marriage.

Results for these five components measuring the effect of development project outputs on fertility through female occupation and income are shown in Table 7.3. The reader is referred to Chapter 2 for the interpretation of the indirect effects explained by the model. We will concentrate on the discussion of the difference between the total effect and the indirect effect of these development projects explained by the model.

Table 7.3 Decomposition of the total effect of development projects on fertility in Sri Lanka

Development program	Total (1)	Indirect (2)	Spurious (3)	Residual I (4)	Residual II (5)
1. Guaranteed price scheme	-0.124	-0.0045	-0.0391	-0.0019	-0.0785
2. Land settlement	0.024	-0.0059	-0.0189	0.0108	0.0380
3. Rural electrification	-0.103	0.0031	0.0319	-0.0001	-0.1380
4. 1 and 3	-0.153	-0.0020	0.0079	-0.0304	-0.1285
5. 1 and 2	-0.016	-0.0073	0.0070	-0.0171	0.0014
6. 2 and 3	-0.086	-0.0061	-0.0178	-0.0153	-0.0468

Note: See text for explanation. Indirect effect explained by the model through occupation and income of wife and the use of family planning. Spurious effect due to the association of project with duration of marriage and female education; Residual I refers to lack of specification of determinants of and measurement errors associated with the use of family planning; and Residual II refers to the lack of specification of proximate determinants of and measurement errors associated with the indicator of fertility.

As mentioned in Chapter 1, the total effects of all the different projects on fertility are significant and in the expected direction except for the land settlement schemes which tend to increase fertility rather than to decrease it. In comparison to the indirect effects explained by the model, the magnitude of residual due to lack of specification of indirect determinants is quite substantial. One of the indirect determinants not included in the model might be the change in the balance between the cost of and benefit from children derived by parents. We assumed that the effect of development projects on this factor is likely to be transmitted through the effect of project outputs on occupation and income. Other factors affecting use of contraception not included in the model might be accessibility or availability of family planning methods in the villages included in the study. The development projects under consideration, however, cannot be assumed to have any direct impact on these factors.

The second residual term relating to the lack of specification of the proximate determinants is much higher than the residual arising due to lack of specification of indirect determinants. Proximate determinants not included in some models are the incidence and length of breastfeeding, age at marriage and induced abortion. Reliable data on induced abortion simply was not obtainable so there is no way to assess the magnitude of the contribution this variable would have made to the total indirect effects. It might be expected, however, to be a more important factor in Thailand where the rate is estimated to be considerably higher than in Sri Lanka. The effect of age at marriage would be expected to be minimal since the studies are not dealing with cumulative fertility but with fertility within the short period of five years. What is really missing is the information on breastfeeding which suppresses fertility. The effect of development projects on fertility through this channel can be positive or negative depending upon the effect of development project on occupation and income and depending upon the effects of these factors on breastfeeding. In a number of cases this effect is likely to be positive if one assumes that higher income is associated with lower incidence of breastfeeding, and that development projects increase income. If our assumption is correct, the inclusion of breastfeeding would have further raised the absolute magnitude of the residual term denoted by item 5.

The Thai studies on irrigation and electrification included the indicators of desired family size and breastfeeding in their analysis.

However, the effects explained by the links specified in Chapters 3 and 4 were also relatively small, implying a large residual category even in these two studies.

The main explanation of getting such a large residual category has to involve the measurement of family planning use and fertility. The fertility measure is based on the number of births which took place during five years prior to interview. Such a measure, by definition, will be affected considerably by the stochastic nature of the event—birth. In fact, the percentage of variance explained in this measure of fertility by a host of proximate and indirect determinants is rarely high. The use of family planning method referred to the current use, and was measured by a dummy variable. A better measure of use incorporating some indicator of duration of its use during the period under investigation would, perhaps, increase the path coefficient from family planning to fertility. It would also increase the magnitude of the path coefficients from occupation/income to family planning use. These increases would raise the magnitudes of indirect effects explained by the model and would lower the magnitudes of both the residual terms. Unfortunately, none of the studies collected data on the duration of family planning use.

Interaction Effect. Assuming that the effect of development project outputs on fertility is indirect, a second type of effect can arise due to some interaction between the community-level output of a project and the individual-level characteristics in influencing the individual fertility behavior. The question addressed by this effect is: Does the presence of a development project (e.g. rural electrification) at the community level affect the relationship between individual characteristics (income or occupation) and fertility? Entwisle, *et al.* (1984) illustrated the importance of this effect in their analysis for rural Thailand in which they showed that the density of family planning services modified the relationship between fertility preferences and contraceptive use.

The authors of the Sri Lanka study compared six regimes of development projects in terms of the net effects of occupation on income, and the net effects of occupation and income on the use of family planning methods, and the net effect of family planning on recent fertility. In these comparisons, couples living in areas without any of these project inputs were used as reference. These comparisons cannot strictly be used to address the question: Does the presence of a development project, for example, rural electrification, modify the relationship between income and the use of family planning? To address this question, an interaction term between a development project (e.g. rural electrification) and income would have to be included in the analysis for each of the six regimes of development projects (see Hermalin, 1985). However, since couples living in rural areas without a development project were included in all the six analyses, the comparisons presented in Chapter 2 can give a good indication about the extent to which the presence of each of the six development regimes modifies the relationships among individual-level variables.

Results presented and discussed in Chapter 2 showed that the relationship between the use of family planning methods and fertility is not modified by the development projects under investigation. The beta coefficients in all the six models measuring this effect varied between -0.14 and -0.17. However, the effect of occupation on income as well as the effects of these two factors on the use of family planning methods were not the same for each of the six regimes of development projects whether one considered male characteristics or female characteristics. Since these differential relationships among individual characteristics were used in estimating the indirect effects of outputs of each of the development projects and their combinations, very little can be added by further elaboration of these interaction effects.

Other factors included in these models were education and the duration of marriage. Beta coefficients measuring the net effects of these factors on other individual characteristics were not shown in Chapter 2. These coefficients indicate that the development project outputs at the community level do not modify the effect of (male or female) education on occupation, income, and the use of family planning methods.

Since the six development project regimes considered by the Sri Lanka study affect occupation and income of both males and females, these projects also modify the relationships between occupation and income and their effects on the use of family planning methods. Since these projects do not affect education, they, perhaps, do not modify the relationship between education and the use of family planning methods.

The presence or absence of an interaction effect cannot be ascertained in the two Thai studies on the effects of rural electrification and irrigation. These effects, if any, are implicitly included in estimating the indirect effects of project outputs on fertility because villages and households which did not benefit from the project outputs were included in the analysis for estimating the net effects of individual characteristics on the desired family size and on the proximate determinants included in the models.

Strength of the Effect of Development Projects on Fertility. As mentioned above, the effect of a development project on fertility can be measured by the correlation coefficients between the indicator of project output and the indicator of fertility. The magnitude of this correlation coefficient indicates the strength of the total effect. How should the strength of this relationship be evaluated? Should development project outputs show any *direct* effect on fertility? These are some of the questions addressed in this section.

Working within the conceptual framework described earlier, it would be unrealistic to expect any direct effect of development project outputs on fertility, if the model is adequately specified. In any empirical analysis, even the household- or the individual-level socioeconomic factors should not show any effect on actual fertility after controlling for the relevant intermediate or proximate variables. Any direct effect of, for example, female education on an indicator of fertility would simply imply that either all the proximate factors are not included in the model or they are not properly measured. If this assertion is accepted, then it follows that macro interventions in terms of development projects cannot show any direct effect on indicators of actual fertility after controlling for the effects of the household- and the individual-level socioeconomic characteristics and the proximate variables. The absence of a significant independent effect of community variables (e.g. rural electrification or village school) on fertility in a number of studies has been erroneously interpreted as indicating no effect of community variables on individual fertility behavior. Such results should be interpreted to indicate that the model is completely specified.

Can the development projects have independent effects on the measures of demand for children? Assuming that the demand for children is adequately measured, it is conceivable that development project outputs can affect the demand for children by changing childbearing incentives or by creating a demand for consumer goods and social services. For example, the presence of a school in the village by keeping children in schools may contribute to a decrease in the utility of children by reducing their labor inputs. This in turn may reduce the demand for children without changing parents' income. Other infrastructural facilities like rural electrification can create demand for consumer goods which in turn may create a demand to reduce family size. Most of the effect of development outputs on childbearing incentives, however, would result from changes in economic and social structures. Without such changes, for example, high demand for child labor may result in high drop-out rates from schools rather than a desire for smaller families. Thus, the development project outputs are unlikely to substantially reduce the desired family size directly, i.e. independent of the effects transmitted through changes in economic and social structures.

In empirical analysis, one way to evaluate the strength of a relationship is to assess whether or not it is statistically significant. Beyond this, the following comparisons can be made to ascertain the relative importance of a particular development project:

1. Compare indirect effects of different development projects explained by the models.
2. Compare total effects of different development projects.
3. Compare the total effect of a development project with the effect of any individual or household factor on fertility.
4. Compare the total effect of a development project with the effect of the use of contraception on fertility.
5. Compare development projects in terms of their effects on social and economic structures.

Comparisons of development projects in terms of their indirect effects have been done in the Sri Lanka study in Chapter 2. These effects cannot be compared with the results of the two Thai studies because the magnitude of the indirect effect explained by a model depends upon the extent of its completeness, which varies across studies in terms of specification of variables.

These various development projects are compared in terms of their total effects on fertility and the use of family planning in Table 7.4. These effects in Thailand are smaller than in Sri Lanka. The reason is as follows. In the Sri Lanka study, the beneficiaries of a development project were compared with the couples living in areas without any development project output. In the two Thai studies, both the beneficiaries and non-beneficiaries living in rural areas with irrigation (or electrification) were compared with couples living in areas without irrigation (or electrification). The macro-level intervention will affect micro-level behavior only if couples actually benefit from this intervention. There might be a spill-over effect on others not directly benefiting from the project output, but this effect will certainly be smaller than the effect on beneficiaries. If both beneficiaries and non-beneficiaries of a macro-level intervention are included in measuring the effect of this intervention, as is done in the two Thai studies, its magnitude will be the average of the effects on beneficiaries and non-beneficiaries. This average magnitude will depend upon the proportion of couples who actually benefit from the intervention, and the magnitude will be lower than the magnitude of the effect upon actual beneficiaries. This will not be a problem if all couples living in an area benefit equally from a macro-level intervention, which is rarely the case.

Table 7.4 Effect of development programs on use of family planning and fertility in Sri Lanka and Thailand

Development program	Family planning *r*	Fertility observed *r*
Sri Lanka:		
1. Guaranteed price scheme	0.04	-0.124
2. Land settlement	-0.02	0.024
3. Rural electrification	-0.08	-0.103
4. 1 and 3	0.17	-0.153
5. 1 and 2	0.17	-0.016
6. 2 and 3	0.14	-0.086
Thailand:		
Electrification	0.08	-0.065
Irrigation	0.04	-0.048

r : Observed correlation coefficient. It measures the total effect of a particular program.

The total effect of development project outputs on the use of family planning methods and recent fertility are compared with the respective effects of individual factors and in case of fertility with the effect of the use of family planning. Instead of showing all correlation coefficients, the averages of the absolute magnitudes of these correlation coefficients of individual factors (e.g. education, occupation, and income) with the use of contraception and recent fertility are shown for comparison purposes. Results are shown in Table 7.5. In terms of the absolute magnitude, the program effect on the use of contraception compares favorably with the effects of individual factors in all cases except for two projects: land settlement and the guaranteed price scheme treated separately.

Table 7.5 Comparison of the effect of development programs with the effects of other variables on the use of family planning and recent fertility in Sri Lanka and Thailand

Development program	Correlation coefficients: Use of contraception		Recent fertility		
	Project output (1)	Average* (2)	Project output (3)	Contraceptive use (4)	Average* (5)
Sri Lanka:					
1. Guaranteed price scheme	0.04	0.12	-0.12	-0.19	0.14
2. Land settlement	-0.02	0.12	0.02	-0.23	0.10
3. Rural electrification	-0.08	0.16	-0.10	-0.23	0.07
4. 1 and 3	0.17	0.13	-0.02	-0.21	0.13
5. 1 and 2	0.17	0.10	-0.15	-0.25	0.11
6. 2 and 3	0.14	0.11	-0.09	-0.23	0.13
Thailand:					
Electrification	0.08	0.07	-0.07	-0.01	0.03
Irrigation	0.04	0.03	-0.05	-0.05	0.03

* Columns (2) and (5) show averages of correlation coefficients without considering their signs. In the Sri Lanka study, six characteristics for which averages are calculated include education, occupation and income of male and female separately. In the Thai study of electrification, education and occupation of males and females and household income are included in calculating averages. In the Thai study of irrigation, wife's education, occupation of male and female, and household income are included for these averages.

In terms of the effect of development project outputs on recent fertility, the absolute magnitudes compare quite favorably with the effects of the individual-level factors and even with the effect of the use of contraception. These comparisons do not imply that the development projects considered here are as important as the use of contraception in reducing fertility but they certainly provide a reason to pause before concluding that the effect of development projects on fertility is small or irrelevant or disappointing.

The actual relevance of development projects can perhaps be judged only in terms of their impacts on social and economic structures. The results presented in Table 7.6 show that these effects without a doubt are quite substantial in all cases.

Appropriate Level of Analysis

Should the macro-level intervention be linked with the micro-level reproductive fertility behavior or should it be linked with the macro-level indicator of fertility? The answer, of course, would depend upon the purpose of the study. If the interest is in the understanding of the mechanisms through which the macro-level intervention can affect micro-level fertility behavior, then the multi-level analysis approach is appropriate. But if the interest is in differentiating communities then the traditional ecological analyses would be more appropriate (see for example, Cutright, 1983, for countries as the unit of analysis; Jain, 1985, for states within India as the unit of analysis; and Hermalin, 1975, for smaller administrative areas in Taiwan as the unit of analysis).

Bulatao & Lee (1983) listed forty questions on the agenda for research. One of these referred to: What variations in institutional and community settings are consistently and reliably related to higher or lower fertility? In their expansion of this question, they suggest that 'It is also advisable, however, to have some research that begins at the other end, not with individual or households models, but with types of institutional and community settings, distinguishing and cataloguing them and determining which are linked to differences in fertility.' Bulatao and Lee did not specify whether they were referring to fertility differences among individuals or among communities. If all individuals exposed to one type of community setting are equally affected by it then it is immaterial whether the reference is in the explanation of fertility

Table 7.6 Effects of development programs on occupation and income in Sri Lanka and Thailand

Development Program	Occupation: Non-Agricultural Male		Occupation: Non-Household Female		Income: Male		Income: Female		Income: Household	
	r	ß	*r*	ß	*r*	ß	*r*	ß	r	ß
Sri Lanka:										
1. Guaranteed Price Scheme	-0.38	-0.38*	0.44	0.44*	0.42	0.39*	0.35	0.01		
2. Land Settlement	-0.47	-0.47*	0.29	0.28*	0.32	0.32*	0.29	0.04*		
3. Rural Electrification	0.34	0.28*	-0.02	0.04	0.39	0.21*	0.15	0.13*		
4. 1 and 3	-0.05	-0.08*	0.01	0.06*	0.70	0.63*	0.19	0.15*		
5. 1 and 2	-0.47	-0.47*	0.43	0.41*	0.25	0.24*	0.40	0.06*		
6. 2 and 3	-0.31	-0.35*	0.44	0.46*	0.70	0.62*	0.43	0.13*		
Thailand:										
Electrification	0.26	0.08**	0.24	0.08**					0.13	0.01
Irrigation	0.07	0.04**	0.06	0.05**					0.06	0.10**

r: Observed correlation coefficient. It measures the total effect of a particular program.

ß: Standardized regression coefficients show the net effect of a program.

1. In the Sri Lanka study, the effect of male (or female) education is controlled for male (or female) occupation; and the effects of both education and income are controlled for income.
2. In the Thailand study of electrification, the effects of village availability of health station and irrigation, and household use of electricity and wife's education are controlled for both male and female occupations; the effects of these variables and occupation of both male and female are controlled for household income.
3. In the Thai study of irrigation, the effects of lengths of time the irrigation project has been in the village, village availability of electrification, health station, and school; and the effects of the size of landholding, female education, and participation in the irrigation project are controlled for both the occupation variables. The effect of these variables along with the occupation of the spouse are controlled for the household income.

* $p < 0.01$ ** $p < 0.05$

differences among individuals or among communities. Both will be the same. However, it is rarely the case. Under most circumstances, all individuals exposed to an institutional setting are not equally affected. Hence, the type of question quoted above can be addressed only by linking macro-level factors with the aggregated index of fertility.

Four of the five research studies included in this book collected village level data and attempted a traditional ecological level of analysis of development impacts upon fertility with the village as the unit of analysis. These activities were undertaken following several workshops conducted with the researchers to identify further areas of analysis. However, the results of this analysis for all four studies proved unreliable and have not been included in the individual chapters. The reasons for this are as follows: First, in cases where village level data were not available on a particular variable, the data were obtained from an aggregation of the household data from the village. In all studies the number of households sampled per village was too small for aggregation to provide a reliable measure of a village level variable. Second, the number of villages in the samples were too small resulting in an insufficient number of observations in variable cells for analysis. Third, even in studies where the number of villages could be considered adequate for analysis, the small population sizes of villages further reduced the reliability of the village birth rates based upon these populations. Finally, the village birth rates are also affected by underregistration of births which has been a chronic problem in village registration systems in most developing countries.

A brief illustrative example from one of the study data sets serves to demonstrate the effect upon an ecological analysis when these latter problems are not taken into account. Table 7.7 presents the results of a multiple regression analysis of village level birth rates on selected village level development variables. These findings would appear to indicate that 20 percent of the fertility variation among villages is accounted for by these variables. Moreover, the village-level availability of irrigation, electrification and health station show a significant negative relationship with fertility net of the effect of the other selected variables. A simple listing of the birth rates, however, calculated from the villages for each province in the study by the size of the irrigation system indicates that this conclusion would be highly suspect (See Table 7.8). Given that the birth rate in the region from which these data were obtained was around 32, it is quite apparent that the rates reported, particularly in the 'medium' and 'small' categories of irrigation size, are substantially underestimated. Admittedly, it could be argued that if these estimates were uniformly underestimated, the results of the regression analysis could be valid. However, this is not the case and yet the regression analysis still indicates a significant negative effect of irrigation, electrification and health station on fertility.

Table 7.7 Multiple regression analysis of average birth rate upon selected development indicators at the village level

Independent variables	Regression coefficient b
1. Length of time irrigation system in the village	-0.616*
2. Length of time village has had electricity	-0.163*
3. Length of time village has had a health station	-8.549*
4. Utilization of irrigation system	2.342
5. Participation in irrigation system	-1.492
6. Type of village road	1.239
7. Availability of school	-2.494
Constant =	32.82
R^2 =	0.20

* Significant at 0.01.
Note: Variables 1, 2 and 3 are measured in single years; 4, 6 and 7 are dummy variables; and variable 5 is measured on a four point scale.

The above example is intended to illustrate the problems encountered in utilizing ecological analysis in the impact studies. This illustration does not negate the importance of ecological analysis, but highlights the shortcoming of the approach when utilized on data of poor quality and high unreliability. Some of the problems can be minimized by increasing the sample size, i.e., the number of villages as well as the number of households per village, which of course will increase the cost of data collection. Other problems associated with the deficiencies of vital registration systems cannot be resolved in the absence of complete enumeration of the villages included in this study.

Table 7.8 Average birth rate per 1,000 population by size of irrigation project at the village level

Province Number	Size of Irrigation Large	 Medium	 Small	 None
	Rate	Rate	Rate	Rate
1	35.64	13.48	10.08	27.03
2	28.68	(6.76)*	37.37	29.94
3	(6.22)*	20.61	(2.53)*	(17.93)*
4	30.54	26.99	13.24	39.60
5	(7.22)*	(2.84)*	(2.99)*	45.93
6	23.48	(9.92)*	(5.06)*	(59.41)*
7	NS	23.12	(6.15)*	29.47
8	NS	(3.62)*	(9.31)*	23.75
9	NS	(5.70)*	(2.33)*	39.49
10	NS	(15.52)*	60.90	29.28
11	NS	NS	18.74	28.38
12	NS	28.97	19.42	18.35
13	NS	(12.20)*	16.67	31.74
14	NS	(12.81)*	15.32	22.77
15	NS	38.52	13.63	36.70
16	NS	NS	19.90	(15.90)*
Total	20.92 (N=20)	17.42 (N=20)	17.49 (N=20)	31.40 (N=40)

NS = No sample in the province
* Three villages or less

Implications for Future Research

The purpose of the fertility impact studies is to measure actual changes in fertility attributable to inputs provided through a development project. The outcome of such studies can provide useful information in the planning process. The results are unlikely to be used to reject a development project because most of these projects can be adequately justified on the basis of their primary objective alone. However, the outcome of impact studies can generate guidelines for assigning higher priority to some development projects on the basis of their anticipated antinatalistic effects and, more importantly, they can be useful in improving the design of a particular project in order to enhance its antinatalistic effect. The utility of this type of research can be further enhanced by concentrating on new projects carefully selected according to criteria specified in this section. Although prospective studies are expensive and difficult to carry out, we believe such studies can be much more useful than the cross-sectional type of studies. The outcome of such studies can be further improved if they are conducted in areas with a good vital registration system.

The fertility impact studies can be done for completed projects, on-going projects, and new projects. For completed projects, by definition, the measurement of fertility change would be based on a retrospective assessment. For the on-going projects, the assessment of fertility change could be based on a combination of retrospective and prospective techniques. The main problem with such projects is the lack of availability of baseline information about fertility levels, differentials, and patterns for the geographic area covered by the project. This limits the scope of the study. One alternative is natural experiments, which involves identification of control areas in which such developmental inputs were not provided but which were similar to the selected areas in all other respects. These opportunities are very rare. The new projects provide an opportunity to set up prospective studies. Experimental design—natural or planned—or statistical control can be used to isolate changes attributable to the project outputs. The studies presented in this book had to be based on the completed projects because of the time and monetary constraints. Considering this experience and methodological issues involved, we recommend the selection of new projects for undertaking the fertility impact studies.

Criteria for Selecting Development Projects for Fertility Impact Studies

Development project outputs affect fertility indirectly by first influencing the community and household environments in which decisions about family size are made. In the mid 1970s, it was assumed that most of the development projects do influence these decisions. However, the studies included in this book and other work done since then have demonstrated that all development projects do not have measurable impacts upon those factors which affect these decisions about family size. It is therefore important to undertake future studies of this type for new development projects selected on the basis of their potential impacts on those factors which are believed to influence decisions about family size. Among the studies presented in this book no such criteria were applied for selection of development projects for analysis. Therefore, it is important that in future research studies the selection of development projects be made on the basis of certain criteria which would maximize the potential for the project's impact on fertility (See Jain, 1980). These criteria would include the following:

1. Purpose of Project

Here, the intention is to select a project that is not too far removed from the ultimate outcome—fertility. If the project is too far removed from fertility, it would be very difficult to project or measure its fertility impact because many intervening steps and linkages cannot be identified. It will be useful to select projects that are organized to directly affect people and exclude those projects which transmit benefits to people *primarily* through sub-grants to other organizations or through training of civil servants. The benefits of such projects at the individual family level would be diluted and the time frame during which such benefits are likely to accrue would be extended.

2. Type of Project

Development projects can be grouped into the following categories depending upon their nature, inputs, and primary objectives:

- Provision of inputs related to intensification of agriculture such as irrigation, credit, seeds, and fertilizer.
- Improvements in the existing infrastructure through rural electrification, motorable road, and transportation and communication.
- Provision of social services related to education, health and nutrition, and water and sanitation.

A fourth category would include those projects which are implemented to directly affect fertility, for example, by improving the accessibility of family planning methods. Evaluation of these projects already consists of their impact on the use of contraception and, therefore, these types of projects are not included in the general classification of development projects.

To further narrow the selection process, it would be useful to concentrate on those development projects that are especially designed to influence those social, economic, and cultural factors that are believed to affect the fertility behavior of couples by changing the demand structure for children, that is, by creating a demand to reduce fertility. Selection of these factors will have to be based upon the existing knowledge concerning the indirect or background determinants of fertility in a country.

3. Geographic Coverage: National vs. Sub-national

Some projects are organized at the national level and others at the sub-national level. It would be preferable to select projects organized at the sub-national level in a well-defined geographical area, because the identification of developmental outputs and their effects on changes in fertility behavior would be more feasible in smaller administrative units. Projects organized at the national level and the area covered by such projects are usually very large and it may be very difficult to link specific project outputs to the potential or actual benefits at the individual family level.

4. Population of the Area Covered by the Project

It will be useful to select projects that cover geographic areas with a population of about 50,000 people. Assuming a birth rate of about 30 per 1,000 population, such projects will provide a reasonable population base to detect non-random changes in fertility. For projects which cover geographic areas with 5 to 10,000 people it may not be feasible to separate changes in the birth rate attributable to project inputs from changes in the birth rate due to random fluctuations or due to deficiencies in data collection.

5. Research and Evaulation Plan

It will be useful to select projects which incorporate research plans to evaluate their intended or direct effects on social and economic structures. This will make it more feasible to extend the evaluation plan to incorporate fertility as one of its dimensions.

In addition to using the above criteria, first priority should be assigned to select those geographic areas where there exists a good vital registration system. New projects selected according to these criteria would provide an opportunity for setting up prospective studies to measure the effects of project outputs on fertility. Ideally, to assess the effects of development project outputs on fertility, one would like to set up an experimental design similar to those used in agriculture to study the effect of a treatment on yield per hectare. Individual couples or small homogenous geographic units (villages/communities) can be used as units to set up an experimental design. Since inputs provided through development projects are organized at an aggregate geographic level, villages or communities might be preferable to the individual couples for setting up an experimental design.

Let us denote communities in which developmental inputs (treatment) are provided as 'experiments.' One would then like to identify 'controls' for these communities. In an experimental design, communities should be randomly assigned to the experimental and control groups. In practice, it is rarely possible to provide developmental inputs on a random basis. The experimental and control communities, therefore, have to be matched on other confounding factors, such as population size, distance from the nearest urban or market center, presence or absence of a primary school, health facilities, and family planning services. These two sets of communities, then, have to be followed prospectively.

Deficiencies of experimental designs as they are applied in social science research, however, must also be recognized. That is, the problems associated with the measurement of inputs and outputs and the control of the external factors in experimental designs, for example, in the field of agriculture, are quite different than the problems associated with an experimental design in fertility-related social science research. Owing to other confounding factors not included in the original list of variables used for matching, one may not be able to estimate the fertility effects of the specific developmental outputs at the end of the experimental design. It is, therefore, important to pay special attention to the selection of factors on which two sets of communities are matched.

A less strict but more practical study will consist of selecting a development project, using it to identify geographic areas in which inputs are to be provided through this project, and monitoring these inputs as well as those provided through other projects. Observed changes in demographic and non-demographic factors can then be decomposed into components attributable to specific project inputs and components attributable to the external factors. This would require a baseline survey, monitoring of inputs and a follow-up survey. Implementation of these surveys will be easier for those projects which contemplate evaluating the intended effects on non-demographic factors such as income and employment. For these projects, one may simply have to add a fertility module consisting of questions about fertility, attitudes about family size, age at marriage, use of contraception, abortion and breastfeeding. Fertility indicators in most cases will be based on current fertility, that is, fertility experience during a three to five year period. It will be important to collect information about the durations of contraceptive use, breastfeeding, postpartum amenorrhea and abstinence. The information about these durations will increase the explanatory power of the model.

The following three issues are important to consider while finalizing the evaluation plan:

a. Whether and to what extent the observed social and economic changes and, therefore, the resulting fertility changes, can be attributed to the project inputs?
b. Whether, at what level of aggregation and with what accuracy, social, economic and fertility changes can be measured?
c. What type of fertility-related information should be collected?

Need for Surrogate Indexes of Fertility Change

In most developing countries, registration systems of vital events are deficient, systems to collect data from a sizeable population on a longitudinal basis are quite expensive to set up and maintain, and information about fertility behavior collected retrospectively has its own problems and deficiencies. The estimates of annual birth rates in many family planning projects have been found to fluctuate erratically from year to year due, perhaps, to deficiencies in the data, seasonal fluctuations in births, and population size of the small geographic units (villages) included in the study. Under these circumstances, it has rarely been possible to establish fertility levels before and after the program implementation and thereby to determine fertility changes in a short period of three to five years. It has been even more difficult to decompose the observed fertility change, if any, into various components that can be attributed to:

1. the developmental inputs;
2. the family planning program inputs;
3. changes in other factors, such as age at marriage, age and sex distribution, breastfeeding and abstinence; and
4. deficiencies in data collection.

These have been some of the major methodological problems faced by researchers interested in assessing the impact of family planning projects on fertility and remain some of the major problems in assessing the fertility impact of development projects as well. In both cases, the end variable is the same. The difference is that instead of searching for a causal factor from family planning inputs, the focus, in the present case, is on developmental inputs. In this sense, many of the methodological problems in assessing the fertility impact of development projects are similar to those researchers have faced while assessing the impact of family planning projects on fertility. There are many additional problems in this particular instance, because the impact of development on fertility is indirect. In the case of family planning projects, the attention sometimes shifts to assessing the impact upon various surrogate indexes—for example, the number of births averted, acceptance rates, continuation rates, contraceptive prevalence rates, and couple-years of protection—instead of measuring the impact upon actual fertility. These surrogate indexes make very little sense in assessing the fertility impact of development projects. Some alternate surrogate indexes will therefore have to be developed. These might include such factors as costs and benefits of children, familial institutions, and preferred family size. The measurement of changes in these factors is also not free of methodological problems.

Alternatively, one can assess the impacts of development projects on those intervening variables which are believed to be associated with changes in demand for children, use of contraception, and fertility. These may include such key factors as *infant and child mortality*, *child labor and schooling*, *female education*, and *women's income and employment*. The selection of these key factors can be made on the basis of certain assumptions about the socioeconomic or indirect determinants of fertility. These assumptions can be expanded, modified, and revised as more information about the determinants of fertility become available. In the meantime, a useful area of further investigation is to study the 'determinants of key socioeconomic determinants' of fertility.

Research on project-specific impact on and determinants of these known, or presumed, key determinants of fertility would help to identify ways to modify them through development policies and programs in a way that potential changes in these determinants are consistent with demographic objectives. For example, family planning research has demonstrated that provision of family planning services is an important input but it does not necessarily lead to the acceptance of family planning methods under all circumstances. Similarly, provision of educational facilities through schools is an important input but it is not adequate to improve educational attainment, especially of female children. Assuming that schooling among female children will modify their parents' fertility behavior and their own fertility when they go through their reproductive period, research on the effects of development projects upon female educational attainment will help to identify factors, other than provision of schools, that impinge upon female educational attainment. This type of research will bring to the surface such obstacles as female drop-out rates from school and potential conflicts between demand for child labor and their schooling, if any. This will also prompt development planners to think of alternative ways of reducing such potential conflicts in order to decrease child labor and increase female educational attainments, which in turn will modify the fertility of their parents and the subsequent fertility behavior of these females.

The work in the area of women's role in development already incorporates research activities on the impact of development projects on female employment and income. Extension of this work to analyze the effects of development projects upon women's roles, and the effects these roles have upon infant and child mortality, investment to improve the education of their children and eventually on their fertility intentions and behavior would further strengthen the assumption underlying the ongoing work which states that 'Women's degree of participation in the development process is a crucial determinant of their demographic behavior.'

References

Berelson, Bernard, 1978. 'Prospects and Programs for Fertility Reduction: What? Where?' *Population and Development Review*, **4** (4), pp.579–616.

Bulatao, Rodolfo A., and Lee, Ronald D., (eds.) with Paula E. Hollerbach and John Bongaarts, 1983. *Determinants of Fertility in Developing Countries: A Summary of Knowledge*. Vols 1 and 2, New York, Academic Press.

Casterline, John B. (ed.), 1985a. *The Collection and Analysis of Community Data*. Voorburg, Netherlands, International Statistical Institute.

Casterline, John B., 1985b. 'The Macro Determinants of Fertility: Lessons from the WFS Experience.' Paper presented at the 1985 Annual Meeting of the Population Association of America, Boston.

Cutright, Phillips, 1983. 'The Ingredients of Recent Fertility Decline in Developing Countries.' *International Family Planning Perspectives* **9** (4), pp.101–9.

Entwisle, Barbara, Hermalin, Albert I., Kamnuansilpa, Peerasit & Chamratrithirong, Apichat, 1984. 'A multilevel model of family planning availabiity and contraceptive use in rural Thailand.' *Demography*, **21** (4), pp.559–74.

Freedman, Ronald, Fan, Tze-Hwa, Wei, Sou-Pen, & Weinberger, Mary Beth, 1977. 'Trends in Fertility and in the Effects of Education on Fertility in Taiwan, 1961–74.' *Studies in Family Planning*, **8** (1), pp.11–18.

Freedman, Ronald, 1985. 'Summary Observations on the WFS Seminar on Collection and Analysis of Data on Community and Institutional Factors,' in J. Casterline, (ed.) 1985. *The Collection and Analysis of Community Data*. Voorburg, Netherlands, International Statistical Institute.

Hermalin, Albert I., 1975. 'Regression Analysis of Areal Data,' in C. Chandrasekaran & Albert I. Hermalin (eds.) *Measuring the Effect of Family Planning Programs on Fertility*. Belgium, Ordina Editions.

Hermalin, Albert I., 1985. 'Integrating individual and community data in the study of contraceptive behavior,' in J. Casterline, (ed.), 1985. *The Collection and Analysis of Community Data*. Voorburg, Netherlands, International Statistical Institute.

Jain, Anrudh K., 1978. 'Some Issues Pertinent to the Assesment of Demographic Impacts of Development Policies,' *Working Paper No. 1*, International Programs, The Population Council, New York.

Jain, Anrudh K., 1980. 'Possibilities for Fertility Impact Assessment of USAID Assisted Projects in Thailand.' *Working Paper*. Bangkok, The Population Council, Regional Office for South and East Asia.

Jain, Anrudh K., 1985. 'The Impact of Development and Population Policies on Fertility in India.' *Studies in Family Planning* **16** (4), pp.181–98.

Stoeckel, John, 1979. 'An Overview of Methodological Issues in Fertility and Development Research.' Paper presented at the seminar on 'Regional Fertility and Development in Thailand.'

The Population Council, 1981. *Proceedings: Workshop on Methodological Approaches to Research on Fertility Impacts of Development*. Bangkok, The Population Council, Regional Office for South and East Asia.

Index

DATE DUE
